Knolly!
with all the best —
Don Chidsey

6 Oct, 1967

THE
GREAT
CONSPIRACY

AARON BURR.

THE
GREAT
CONSPIRACY

*Aaron Burr and His Strange
Doings in the West*

Donald Barr Chidsey

CROWN PUBLISHERS, INC., NEW YORK

BY THE SAME AUTHOR

HISTORICAL

GOODBYE TO GUNPOWDER
THE BIRTH OF THE CONSTITUTION
JULY 4, 1776
VALLEY FORGE
THE BATTLE OF NEW ORLEANS
VICTORY AT YORKTOWN
THE GREAT SEPARATION
THE TIDE TURNS
THE SIEGE OF BOSTON
THE WAR IN THE NORTH

BIOGRAPHY

ELIZABETH I
A Great Life in Brief

JOHN THE GREAT
The Times and Life of John L. Sullivan

THE GENTLEMAN FROM NEW YORK
A Biography of Roscoe Conkling

SIR HUMPHREY GILBERT
Elizabeth's Racketeer

SIR WALTER RALEIGH

MARLBOROUGH
The Portrait of a Conqueror

BONNIE PRINCE CHARLIE
A Biography of the Young Pretender

Contents

THE
GREAT
CONSPIRACY

CHAPTER

1

THE BIGGEST real estate deal in history was made in Paris, and its consequences were world-shaking.

Charles Maurice de Talleyrand-Périgord, an old-line diplomat, all deceit and satiny manners, was out of place in the government of the First Consul of France, that arrogant young Corsican soldier Napoleon Bonaparte, who despised him. But in 1803 Napoleon was not yet used to moving the principalities of Europe around like cards on a table—a practice that takes some training—and he needed this glittering holdover from the royal court, at least for a little while. He cursed Talleyrand, but he kept him on.

Talleyrand was aware that an additional envoy was on his way from the new Republic of the United States to assist the resident ambassador, Robert Livingston. The latter was currently engaged in trying to get Talleyrand, as foreign minister, to agree to terms to buy the city of New Orleans and perhaps West Florida,[1] and to settle American claims against French privateers in the undeclared war just ended. He was aware as well that Livingston was a member of the fading Federalist party in his home state of New York, whereas the newcomer, a man named James Monroe, on the sea right then, was not only a Republican-Democrat [2] but a Virginian as well, and Virginians were not fond of New Yorkers, or the other way about. These facts gave the wily one an excuse to prevaricate—something he loved to do. "Well, since you are about to be superseded anyway"—he would begin; and Livingston would indignantly interrupt, crying that he was *not* to be superseded, only assisted; and Talleyrand would shrug.

Talleyrand's manners were exquisite, his intentions a mystery. *La merde dans un bas de soie* was one of the least unpleasant things his lord and master called him.

Now, on the morning of Monday, April 11, the day after Easter, Talleyrand spread his hands and asked, almost casually: "Would the United States wish to have the whole of Louisiana?"

Livingston was caught off guard. "No," he answered absentmindedly; the United States might conceivably, in time, be interested in the territory north of the Arkansas River, but never in the whole vast stretch of Louisiana.

Then he sat forward suddenly, realizing for the first time what was being offered. The land was stupendous, so big that nobody really knew how far it extended; it was, in fact, five times as big as France itself. This was what was being held out, an empire. Such an acquisition would more than double the size of the United States.

To be sure, Livingston had no authority to dicker for such a princely prize; but it took three months or more to get a question to President Jefferson or to Secretary of State Madison and to receive an answer, and the man behind this oily diplomat Livingston faced, Napoleon Bonaparte, notoriously had a womanlike tendency to change his mind.

Of one thing Livingston could be sure: Talleyrand would never have broached the subject if he had not been commanded to do so. The First Consul was not one to encourage enterprise among his representatives. Napoleon himself must have ordered the sale of Louisiana.

Why?

France was at peace with England, but Napoleon was one who used wars lightly: he could always seem to find another when he needed it. *Il n'y a plus de Pyrénées*, Louis XIV had proclaimed when his grandson was made King of Spain. He was mistaken. Bourbons still sat on the throne at Madrid, but the Pyrenees had not evaporated. Technically, France and Spain were equal allies; but the truth is that they were master and slave. The Spaniards, like everybody else in Europe, were afraid of Bonaparte. He had a little while ago easily forced Spain to cede the whole Louisiana territory back to France—the Retrocession it was called, for France perforce had ceded it to Spain in 1763 at the end of the Seven Years' War. (Britain had declined to accept Louisiana herself, preferring to take the Floridas, which she subsequently ceded back to Spain.) He must have some reason for such a move.

Napoleon could count on the Spanish Navy, such as it was, but even when combined with the French Navy, such as *that* was, it could hardly be expected to beat the British. The British Navy, should England be at war with France, could stopper the neck of the Louisiana territory, the mouths of the Mississippi, any Thursday afternoon, and the rest of that vast land mass would automatically fall. Napoleon (Livingston might have reasoned) until recently no doubt had planned to prevent such a take-over by means of a naval station part way from France to Louisiana—namely, the island of Hispaniola in the West Indies. France owned half of that island, Haiti, and Spain owned the other half, Santo Domingo, which was as good as saying that France owned it all. France, still a bit drunk from its Revolution, had promised all the blacks their freedom forevermore; but Napoleon would have none of this, and ordered slavery reinstated, whereupon the Negroes revolted. Their leader, Toussaint l'Ouverture, was lured out of the jungle by vows that he would never be imprisoned—and then was sent to a dank cell in France, where he was to die of pleuropneumonia; but the blacks fought on. Thousands of Frenchmen fell before them, and thousands more perished of disease. France simply could not afford that kind of bleeding, and the adventure was broken off. Napoleon knew when to quit, as he had shown in Egypt. Without Hispaniola, however, he could never hope to protect Louisiana. Could it be then that he would rather see it go to the United States than fall to Great Britain? Livingston must have thought this possible, even probable. Also, Napoleon could use some extra cash, for wars are expensive.

There was a pause. Then Talleyrand protested that of course this was just an idea of his own, nothing official; and Livingston said of course.

Livingston, trying to sound offhand, suggested a price of 20,000,000 livres, provided, he hastened to add, that the spoliation claims, amounting to about 25,000,000 francs, were met.

Talleyrand smiled and changed the subject.

Livingston had a lot to think about. He knew—it was his business to know things like this—that, although the actual retrocession of Louisiana from Spain to France had not yet been consummated, all details were arranged and the deed was as good as done. Talleyrand, earlier in these negotiations, had insisted that it was not France's part to haggle, for, he said, the property after all belonged to Spain, not France; but Livingston knew better, for he had seen a copy of the secret treaty. Livingston knew too that Napoleon had given his solemn assurance that France would not let any other nation get that territory. But the First Consul was a shameless liar, a man who believed that disavowals were all part of the game; who might have asserted, with Swift, that promises and pie-crust were meant to be broken.

Livingston was after Talleyrand again the next morning, raising his unauthorized price; but Talleyrand was cool.

James Monroe by this time was in France—a tall, stooped man with understanding gray-blue eyes and an equable temper—and at one o'clock that Tuesday afternoon he presented himself at Livingston's house. Ill, pale, with legs still shaking from that long sea voyage, he yet was all eagerness to be about the business at hand. A veteran of the Revolution, member of both houses of Congress, and twice the governor of Virginia, he was a youngish man, and of late his ambition had begun to show: it was pretty well understood around Washington that he had his eye on the Presidency.

Had Livingston been able to complete the deal before Monroe's arrival, he would have been given all the praise for it, culminating many months of weary work; but by that same token he might have seen the sale denounced in the Democratic-dominated United States Senate. As it was, if the deal went through, Monroe would get the lion's share of the credit, since the Democrats controlled not only the Presidency and both houses of Congress, but the great majority of the journals as well, and party feeling was very strong.

Nevertheless, these two men worked well together.

That very afternoon, while they were dining, Livingston espied a mutual friend, François, Marquis de Barbé-Marbois, formerly the secretary of legation in the United States and now the French finance minister, who "just happened" to be strolling through the embassy garden. Barbé-Marbois liked Americans; he was married to an American; he would be friendly. Livingston called him in and told him about the conversation with Talleyrand. Barbé-Marbois was not amazed. Napoleon had spoken to him too, and he had some ideas as to price. Monroe, worn out, retired early, but Livingston and Barbé-Marbois talked long and late, and before *he* went to bed the ambassador wrote a long triumphant letter to the secretary of state, claiming full credit for a completed deal.

That was premature. There were to be days, there were to be weeks, of chaffering. The discussions were all *in camera* and no official record was made of them.

Such secrecy was needed. If Spain got wind of these doings she would surely protest. If the French public heard of them—though the French public was not highly esteemed at this time—the howl would be deafening. Napoleon Bonaparte even had trouble among the members of his own family, a notably quarrelsome lot. Two of his brothers, Lucien and Joseph, heard of the negotiations and called upon him at the Tuileries, where they found him in his bath. They remonstrated. They shook their fists and screamed, and he screamed back, splashing them with scented bath water. They made such a din that the only witness, a valet, fainted from fright.

Somehow, eventually, the Americans and Barbé-Marbois came to terms that the First Consul consented to accept.

"We have lived long," Livingston said to Barbé-Marbois and to Monroe, "but this is the noblest work of our lives." [3]

Three conventions were signed April 30 and May 2, and the thing was wrapped up. Marbois had lowered the French price for the land to 60,000,000 francs—he had originally demanded 100,000,000—and the spoliation claims were whittled down to 20,000,000 francs. With interest payments and the assumption of many of the spoliation claims by the United States government, the total price was a little more than $27,260,000, which, calling the Louisiana Purchase about 1,000,000 square miles—as good a guess as any—came to about 4 cents an acre.

Monroe got all the credit.

CHAPTER

2

THE SETTLERS on the western side of the mountains—between Appalachia and the Mississippi—were a separate set of people. They were not like the residents of the East, whence all of them had come, and they were suspicious of those persons. They were the restless of the nation, the adventurous, the misfits. They had gone west for various reasons, some out of plain curiosity, some fleeing from creditors or wives, most perhaps with that pot of gold at the foot of the rainbow splendidly dancing before their eyes.

They were rugged individualists. They shared with the despised easterners a passion for land deals, but that was one of the very few things they did share. New York, Virginia, Massachusetts, Connecticut, and North Carolina had been persuaded to cede to the federal government their rights to enormous tracts of western land, and the states were coming into the Union one by one—Kentucky in 1792, Tennessee in 1796, Ohio in 1803, respectively the fifteenth, sixteenth, and seventeenth (Vermont had been the fourteenth)—but they still believed that they were looked down upon by the easterners, their needs ignored, their aspirations flouted. They were gaining power in Washington, but too slowly to suit their impatient appetites.

Besides, they were not getting their share of the tax money, or so they thought. Those easterners were on a spending spree which the westerners could do nothing to stop. Why, it had cost $3,737,000 to run the country in 1802. What kind of a business administration was that? And how much of it was permitted to cross the mountains?

Congress was flooded with petitions for independence, some of them respectful, many threatening. "The Mississippi is ours by the law of nature," several hundred Ohio Valley settlers wrote, and went on to say that if it was not kept open they would seize the city of New Orleans, "and . . . we will know how to maintain ourselves there."

New Orleans, a small sleepy place, oppressively low, hot, flat, was in all of their minds. It was down in the delta country and controlled the mouths of the Mississippi River. For many thousands of scattered farmers, the river was the only route to a market, and the thought that New Orleans was in the hands of foreigners who might at any time declare it closed to traffic was intolerable to the westerners. Congress ought to do something about it.

Then there was the malodorous matter of the Yazoo claims, essentially a Western affair, though it created more consternation among the Eastern bankers.

Unlike so many of the others, Georgia had never been brought to make over its western lands to the federal government, and it claimed all the territory west to the Yazoo, an obscure river from which the Yazoo Grants got their name. This comprised about 35,000,000 acres, inhabited chiefly by Creeks, Cherokees, Choctaws, and Chickasaws, a scrappy lot, and it also included a great deal of what Spain claimed as

West Florida. It would be ideal cotton land; and cotton, since the recent invention of the gin, had become of overwhelming commercial importance.

In 1789, the state of Georgia, ignoring the Indians and ignoring the Spaniards, had essayed to sell this vast tract to a private company, but there was not enough money behind the buyers, who did not include many sound names, and the deal fell through. In 1795, it was different. The whole expanse was sold to a group of four privately owned land companies for a total of $500,000, or less than 1½ cents an acre.

Immediately there was a yelp of protest, a demand that the sale be set aside as fraudulent. In truth, there had been almost no attempt to conceal the corruption. Legislators who objected to the flagrant bribery were told (by men with cudgels) to go home. Only one man who voted for the grant could prove that he did not own shares in any of the four companies. All of the rest had suddenly become rich.

But the legislature had adjourned, or rather dissolved, and the Yazoo Grants shares already were being sold and resold far from Georgia—indeed, especially in New England, for the largest of the four companies was located in Boston. Money had changed hands.

The indignant citizens of Georgia elected an almost completely new legislature the following year, 1796, and the first act of this body was to declare null and void the sales act of the previous year. They even went so far as to order that act publicly burned; and after some bright person had pointed out that a document inspired from hell should only be ignited by means of power from Heaven, this was done— with a sun lens.

Such ceremonies, however, could not obliterate the fact that, unless the sale stood, hundreds of honest-meaning men would be ruined. The country had gone Yazoo-mad. There were brokers who dealt in nothing else. The average selling price was 14 cents an acre, but a 10,000-acre plot was esteemed small. Millions were at stake.

Did the federal government have the right to intervene and to tell the Georgia legislature that it had acted illegally? This was a matter for the Supreme Court to decide, later. Meanwhile, President Jefferson appointed a board consisting of Secretary of State Madison, Secretary of the Treasury Gallatin, and Attorney General Levi Lincoln, and this board brought in a compromise suggestion that was being considered.

Tempers were frayed, on both sides of the mountains, over the Yazoo Grants scandal.

Among the most dissatisfied of the settlers were those along the Tombigbee. Robert R. Livingston had believed, or pretended to believe, that the Louisiana Purchase included West Florida, but Spain never did relinquish her claim to this territory, and the men along the Tombigbee and the Alabama still were without access to the open sea. The taking of New Orleans didn't do *them* any good.

The Purchase had proved politically embarrassing. Until that time the Democratic-Republican party had been firm in a strict-constructionist policy, insisting that the federal government had only the powers specifically granted to it by the Constitution, whereas the Federalist party stood for a looser interpretation, a stronger central government. Now these positions would be exactly reversed—unless Jefferson was willing to forego this bargain, which he was not. His own personal notion was that the Purchase could be made legal and the Democratic party kept consistent only by means of a Constitutional amendment retroactively giving Congress the power to buy any land it wanted, and he drew up just such an amendment. But there was no time to present it and to have the states ratify it, for word had come from Paris that Napoleon Bonaparte was wavering again and might at any time change his mind and call the whole Purchase off. The acceptance bill, therefore, was rushed through Congress and passed by a strict party vote—90 to 25 in the House, 26 to 5 in the Senate. Even the usually balky "Quids" voted for it.[4]

Considering the pretensions of the Democratic-Republican party, its much-touted preference for local rule, and its horror of government from afar, it is curious that it came up with such a tyrannical administration law for Louisiana. Certainly the new citizens, most of whom were Spanish and residents of New Orleans, did not like it; and it could be significant that the Spanish territorial officials did not go away promptly but lingered for several years, as though expectant of another switch, a return to power, until they were actually *ordered* away by the American governor, when they departed in a huff.

The law broke the Purchase into two parts, north and south, the dividing line being the thirty-third parallel of latitude.[5] The northern part was virtually uninhabited, except by roving bands of Indians. It was called the District of Louisiana, and it was under the one-man rule of Brigadier General James Wilkinson. Wilkinson was also military chief of the southern half, a man in Spanish pay who for years had been taking a $2,000 annual pension from the governor-general of Mexico. The southern part, called the Territory of Orleans, which of course included the city, was in charge of Governor William Charles Cole Claiborne, a rather indeterminate executive who was to be advised by a council of men supplied direct from Washington. The residents of New Orleans, by and large, had nothing to say in their own government. They complained, and loudly, that they were worse off than they had been before.

It was notable that neither Claiborne nor Wilkinson could speak a word of Spanish.

The Louisiana Purchase, in short, did nothing to ease the tension in the land between the mountains and the Mississippi—"the Father of Waters"—but rather tended to increase this. That land was a powder keg that only waited for a spark to set it off. The spark was soon to be supplied.

3

THE TWO highest-priced lawyers in New York caused themselves to be rowed across the North River to the wilderness that was Weehawken early one lovely Wednesday morning in July of 1804. They went separately.

Colonel Aaron Burr and his friend William P. Van Ness got there first, and they left the boatmen in the boat and climbed to a wooded spot a little distance inland, a spot from which they would have had a beautiful view of the river, should they look in that direction; but they were not, this morning, interested in natural scenery. They took off their coats. They paced the level ground, trampling down small bushes, clearing away broken branches.

General Alexander Hamilton came soon afterward. He was accompanied by Nathaniel Pendleton, who carried the guns in a box, and by Dr. David Hosack, who carried a surgeon's bag. Dr. Hosack remained with the boatmen, while the other two climbed to the field.

Everybody bowed to everybody else, and the pistols were produced. The seconds measured the distance: ten paces.

They did not take unnaturally long strides, as was sometimes done in these affairs in order to make the distance
greater, but were scrupulously natural, marching side by side.

The balls were cut, the powder weighed, the pistols
loaded, all of this being done by the seconds while the principals stood a short space away looking in the other direction.

Hamilton's representative won the toss for position and
a second toss for giving the signal to shoot, which would be
the word "Present." The regulations, a four-section cartel
drawn up the previous day, continue: "If one of the parties
fires, and the other hath not fired, the opposite second shall
say one, two, three, fire, and he shall then fire or lose his shot.
A snap or flash is a fire."

This being perfectly understood, the principals went to
their places. It was about seven o'clock.

At a glance you might have taken these duellists to be
twins. They were rather frail men, very dapper in their dark
silk clothes and their clubbed and powdered hair. Alexander
Hamilton stood 5 feet 7, Aaron Burr, 5 feet 6. Burr was
forty-eight years old, Hamilton, forty-seven. Each was a
hero of the Revolution, and each had been an academic
prodigy—Hamilton an honor student at King's College before the war, and Burr, a graduate of the College of New
Jersey [6] at the age of sixteen.

The differences, however, were deep. Burr, a grandson
of Jonathan Edwards, had many generations of roots in continental America, and was a member of a distinctly distinguished family, whereas Hamilton, a bastard, came from an
insignificant West Indian island—Nevis; his father a Scot, his
mother French. Hamilton was quick, intense, sharp, des-
perately sincere, an emotional man; Burr was urbane. Hamilton had a cutting wit; Burr, a quiet sense of the ridiculous.
Hamilton, though he was somewhat rigid in public and af-

fected an icy reserve, tended to wax shrill when excited; Burr, cynically sure of himself, seldom raised his voice.

Each considered himself a gentleman, and was so considered by his friends, otherwise there would have been no meeting this morning in Weehawken. Yet Burr, a member of the so-called Democratic or Republican party, derived his political strength in large part from the unwashed masses, and though he never mixed with them or visited their meeting place, he had virtually invented Tammany Hall. On the other hand, Alexander Hamilton, married to a Schuyler, was an unblushing aristocrat, an economic royalist who despised and distrusted "the people."

Hamilton, a moralist, hated Aaron Burr with a high hot hatred that seemed to feed upon itself, flaming. There was something pathological about it. Burr, a politician not given to expressing personal opinions, probably did not bother much about Hamilton one way or the other—until Hamilton, who sometimes could not keep his mouth shut, got into his, Burr's, way.

Burr, incidentally, was the Vice President of the United States. Hamilton until a little while earlier had been Secretary of the Treasury.

Both men had reached the crest of their attainments and talents and had nowhere else to go but down, though it is not likely that either of them would have admitted this, even to himself.

As the father of a large family, and one who never hesitated to comment caustically upon the shortcomings of others, Alexander Hamilton must have been mortified when recently he had been forced to confess—or believed himself forced to confess—that he had for some time been carrying on an affair with a woman of the town, a Mrs. Reynolds, whose husband blackmailed him. Aaron Burr, on the other hand, never seemed to care what people said about him. He had married the widow of a British Army colonel, the mother of five children, by whom he had but one child, his adored and adoring Theodosia, but Mrs. Burr long since had passed away, and the Vice President's successes with survivors were prodigious. It was whispered that the brothels of New York City were filled with women he had ruined, which was doubtless *something* of an exaggeration. If Burr ever heard this story he would have been amused. He was an even-tempered man with a great gift for pleasure, and in ordinary circumstances would not take the trouble to defend himself.

However, there could be exceptions. When it became clear that, for party reasons, he could not expect to be re-elected Vice President, he was talked into running for governor of New York, a position esteemed only slightly inferior in power and honor to the Presidency itself. This candidacy might have been declared at the instigation of certain members of the moribund Federalist party, who were thinking of breaking off New England, New York, and possibly New Jersey from the rest of the nation. There *could* have been such a deal; it is not certain. What is certain is that Hamilton, himself a Federalist of the deepest dye, opposed Burr's election with a rancor that was fanatical, at last thwarting it.

Even a state the size of New York was not large enough to hold both of these men.

Burr had plenty to pick from. He chose a clipping from the *Albany Register* in which an upstate clergyman told of having heard General Hamilton declare, at a private party, that Colonel Burr was not to be trusted in public office. Hamilton had said worse than this, and many times; but this was all that Burr needed for the present. He sent it to Hamilton by his friend Van Ness, together with a short, impeccably polite request for an explanation.

Hamilton knew what it meant. He was a great man, granted; but when he replied to Burr's note, two days later, it was in a moment of nongreatness. His own letter was evasive, rambling, and querulous. It only muddied the situation. It was not even well written. That was June 20.

There were other notes, carried on Hamilton's part by Judge Pendleton. Burr's waxed sterner, edged with threat, though always technically courteous. Hamilton did not seem to know what to say—or write. He could have got out of it. No public apology had been demanded. But he wrestled with his conscience, steering a shifty course; Burr pressed, as he was obliged to do; and at last a duel was decided upon. That was June 27.

Hamilton requested a delay until the close of Circuit Court, in which he had several cases pending, and Burr acceded to this. The date of July 11 was set.

So for two whole weeks these men went about their respective businesses as though everything was as usual. No word leaked out. They even attended a Society of the Cincinnati dinner and sat close together and still nobody knew.

Now they were face to face on a hill in Weehawken.

The pistols were cocked and handed to the principals. They were huge things, of .56 calibre, 16 inches in length, overall, with 11-inch barrels. Hamilton had brought them. He had borrowed them from his brother-in-law, John Barker Church.[7]

The seconds stepped back.

Hamilton moved his pistol from side to side, squinting along its barrel. He apologized for holding up the proceedings, at the same time muttering something about the light. With his left hand he fished a pair of spectacles out of a coat pocket and placed these upon his nose. Then he nodded to indicate his readiness to go ahead.

AARON BURR SHOOTS ALEXANDER HAMILTON.

"Present!"

Both men fired.[8]

Hamilton's ball went through the branch of a cedar tree at a point about 12½ feet above the ground and about 4 feet off the formal line of fire, to the right.

Burr's ball went into the right side of Hamilton's belly, clipped one of the false ribs, smashed both liver and diaphragm, and lodged in either the first or second lumbar vertebra.

Hamilton stiffened. He went up on his toes, as though about to start a dance. He turned a little to the left and fell on his face.[9]

Pendleton went to him promptly. Burr, the still-smoking pistol dangling at his side, started toward him, a gesture of grief; but Van Ness intervened, leading him away.

The boatmen and Dr. Hosack down by the shore heard the shots, and all three started up the hill. They could be heard coming, though they could not yet be seen.

Van Ness opened an umbrella, brought along for this very purpose—for it was a clear day—and covered Burr's head with this as he led him down to the shore. The idea was that then the boatmen and Dr. Hosack would not be able to swear that Burr had been seen leaving the scene, which was absurd.

At the boat Burr once again balked, crying out that he ought to go back, he might be able to help. Again Van Ness dissuaded him. They were rowed to the foot of Canal Street, Manhattan, and went from there to Burr's town house, Richmond Hill,[10] into which they locked themselves.

"This is a mortal wound, doctor," Hamilton managed to whisper; but he did not say much else.

It was clearly not a case for field treatment, and they carried Hamilton down to the boat. All feeling was leaving his legs, he told them in what voice he could muster, and everything was going gray before his eyes. He was in horrible pain.

A merchant, a good friend, William Bayard, met them on the Manhattan shore. Servants had told him of the setting-forth of the two boats, and he had guessed the rest. Since Hamilton's own home, The Grange, was far to the north of town,[11] the wounded man was taken to Bayard's house, 80-82 Jane Street, where Dr. Hosack started giving him laudanum, more than an ounce at a time, and putting tepid anodyne fomentations on the parts nearest the seat of pain. But the good doctor knew that there was no hope.

The French consul-general in New York, hearing about the business—it was all over town in no time—offered the services of some naval surgeons from a few French frigates in the bay, men who would know about gunshot wounds, and they came, and looked, and shook their heads, agreeing with Dr. Hosack.

The family appeared, weeping. It was an utter shock to them.

In a moment of lucidity Hamilton asked for the bishop of New York, Benjamin Moore, who came. Hamilton asked to have Holy Communion administered to him, but the bishop replied that he would have to think it over. A few hours later the bishop was sent for again, and Hamilton pleaded with him.

"I observed to him," the bishop wrote, "that he must be very sensible of the delicate and trying situation in which I was then placed; that however desireous I might be to afford consolation to a fellow mortal in distress; still, it was my duty as a minister of the gospel, to hold up the law of God as paramount to all other law; and that, therefore, under the influence of such sentiments, I must unequivocally condemn the practice which had brought him to his present unhappy

condition. He acknowledged the propriety of these sentiments, and declared that he viewed the late transaction with
sorrow and contrition. I then asked him, 'Should it please
God, to restore you to health, Sir, will you never be again
engaged in a similar transaction? and will you employ all your
influence in society to discountenance this barbarous custom?'
His answer was, 'That, Sir, is my deliberate intention.'"

The Bishop questioned him further, and at last, convinced, administered the sacrament.

Alexander Hamilton died soon afterward, at about
two o'clock on the afternoon of Thursday, July 12, having
lived thirty-one hours, always in searing pain, after being
shot. And by dying—and this would have amazed the man
himself—he became a martyr.

CHAPTER

4

The hullabaloo was deafening. Preachers denounced; orators thundered; resolutions were passed, all white-hot with indignation. A stranger might have assumed that duelling was a brand-new and barbarous institution suddenly—and forcibly —introduced into these hitherto innocent United States; whereas in truth duelling, or the *thought* of duelling the *threat* of it, were everyday matters. In the West, the duel was a formalization of the brawl, and as such acceptable, even desirable. In the South, it was rampant. A governor of South Carolina published a duelling code, and Charleston had its duelling club after the manner of Heidelberg. Sometimes, of a good morning, there were as many as four or five couples, complete with seconds and surgeons, waiting in line to use the space under the Allard plantation oaks just outside New Orleans.[12] Even in the North the duel was by no means unknown, and men who moved in circles such as Hamilton and Burr moved in, while they regarded it as a serious matter, took the necessity of it for granted. There were laws against the practice in some states, true; but there were laws against so many things, and a gentleman's honor in any event surely was above a commoner's law?

Hamilton in his lifetime never had enjoyed much personal popularity, for he was an arrogant little man with no sense of humor; his political views, always extreme, had been discredited; he was loaded with debts, for his speculations had gone wrong; and he was no longer a power in his own disintegrating party. But now, by the simple process of shooting straight, Burr had made him immortal. Now he was a god.

Much was made of the fact that Hamilton had expressed disapproval of the code duello. This, however, was done just before the confrontation in Weehawken, in a paper of "remarks explanatory" which he wrote in New York some time between June 27, when the challenge was actually accepted, and July 4, the day of the Cincinnati society dinner. This paper was a sort of apology-in-advance, in which he protested that he had nothing to win and everything to lose, that he bore no ill will to Colonel Burr, that he feared to hurt his wife and children and also his creditors, but first of all that "My religious and moral principles are strongly opposed to the practice of Duelling and it would ever give me pain to be obliged to shed the blood of a fellow creature in a private combat forbidden by the laws." Coming from him, this is curious. As a young man he was hotheaded, and he frequently engaged in quarrels—with Washington, among others. Yet it was Washington whom he was defending, or thought he was defending, when he tried to challenge General Charles Lee to a duel shortly after the Battle of Monmouth. His friend and fellow headquarters' aide John Laurens got there first, and it was he who met Lee in the field, a bloodless affair; but Hamilton served as Laurens' second. Later, in 1796, after a quarrel about some letters exposing the blackmail plot against

Hamilton, he was about to challenge James Monroe, who had actually gone so far as to send to him "my friend Colonel Burr" with instructions to make the arrangements. Ironically, on this occasion it was Aaron Burr who brought about a reconciliation.

No, Alexander Hamilton had certainly accepted the code duello, though it could hardly be said that he loved it. A recent tragedy might have colored his thinking on the subject. Three years before the meeting in Weehawken, his oldest child, Philip, a sportive lad fresh out of Columbia, was killed in a duel with a Democratic politician. The shock was so severe that it drove Hamilton's oldest daughter, Angelica, into lunacy, a state that was to continue for the rest of her life. This experience could hardly have endeared the practice to Philip's father.

Burr, to make Hamilton the brighter hero, was pictured in the popular imagination as a cold, calculating crack shot (in the only previous duel Burr had fought, he missed) who with cunning malevolence had lured his rival in law and politics into an illegal encounter in which the odds were all on his side. In fact, the affair had been perfectly aboveboard, everything proper. The seconds, the surgeon, Bishop Moore, and everybody else in any way connected with it made public statements afterward, and as far as *they* were concerned there could not have been a more fair, more honest duel. Still, the public demanded a villain, and Burr was loudly cursed, especially in New England, where the few remaining Federalists cried treason, asserting that the whole thing had been a dastardly political plot; the same men who a little earlier had been decrying Alexander Hamilton now noisily deified him.

In truth, Colonel Burr was not safe in New York City, where there was talk of burning his house, of lynching him.

"Oh Burr, oh Burr, what hast thou done?
Thou hast shooted dead great Hamilton!
You hid behind a bunch of thistle
And shooted him dead with a great hoss pistol!"

Silly in itself, this placard (which had been affixed to Burr's house, Richmond Hill) reflects the conviction of scores of thousands that the duel had been nothing more than a cold-blooded murder. The saintly Hamilton, they averred, had been ambushed.

From this surcharged atmosphere Aaron Burr quietly absented himself when he took a boat to Perth Amboy, New Jersey, where he stayed for a few days at the home of his friend the naval hero Commodore Truxtun.

A coroner's jury in New York—one member was an Isaac Burr, no relation—had proceeded ponderously, and polysyllabically, to find the Colonel guilty of murder, though since this "murder" had not been committed in New York State they could go no further. The jurors also took the trouble to condemn the seconds, Van Ness and Judge Pendleton, who "at the time of Committing the felony and Murder aforesaid feloniously Wilfully and of their Malice aforethought ware present, abetting aiding assisting Comforting and Maintaining the said Aaron Burr to kill and Murder the said Alexander Hamilton in Manner aforesaid." A Grand Jury of New York County went further. It brought in a presentment against Burr on a charge of issuing a challenge in New York State—only a misdemeanor, to be sure, but one that could be heavily punished.

When Burr, in Perth Amboy, learned that the Bergen County Grand Jury in New Jersey had indicted him for murder, he decided to get out of *that* state as well. It would be embarrassing if the Vice President of the United States were picked up as a common criminal. Accompanied, then, only by a friend, Samuel Swartwout, and a Negro boy, a servant, Peter, of whom he was very fond, he rode by back roads to Philadelphia, where he rested for a while at the home of Charles Biddle.

Even there he could not feel altogether safe. There was a chance that the Governor of New Jersey might ask the Governor of Pennsylvania to extradite him on the murder charge; and if he had to face trial, with public opinion in its present state, he was as good as hanged. So he took ship for South Carolina, where he visited his daughter, Theodosia, whose husband, the rich young Joseph Alston, had an estate on the Waccamaw.

Theodosia, named after her mother, was that *rara avis*, a beautiful bluestocking, as erudite as she was easy to look at. It was to her that her father, before going to the field, committed his letters and papers, stipulating that certain letters (from women, of course) should be burned, and that certain servants, among them Peter, should be pensioned.

He was back in Washington that fall for the opening of Congress, having made the trip overland, meeting, on the whole, excellent receptions, especially in Virginia, where he was made much of.

There were many who wondered, often audibly, whether Aaron Burr would have the nerve to take his seat as presiding officer of the United States Senate. Well, he did; and he did it with his accustomed dignity.

Important business was waiting for that august body. Of the three branches of the federal government, Thomas Jefferson *was* the executive, and he controlled both houses of the legislative department by big majorities. The judicial, however, eluded him, even at times defying him. Just before John Adams ceased to be President, he had made sundry judicial appointments—his "midnight appointments" Jefferson called them—and a Senate, largely consisting of lame ducks, had ratified these. The bench, then, unlike the other two branches, was heavily Federalist. Jefferson did not like this. He thought that all three branches should work together. He disapproved most violently of the doctrine of judicial review that the Chief Justice, John Marshall, was inculcating. He did not believe that even the Supreme Court had the right to declare an act passed by Congress unconstitutional. The Constitution itself specified only that Supreme Court justices should hold their offices "during good behavior," so that the President had no power to discharge them. Nevertheless, he tried, come-willy-come-nilly, to get them out. He caused Judge John Pickering of New Hampshire to be impeached, chiefly on charges of drunkenness and foul language on the bench. Aaron Burr had presided at Pickering's trial, and the man was found guilty, but this was a comparatively minor matter, for Pickering had been only a federal District Court judge and certifiably insane to boot. To convict Samuel Chase would be another thing.

Chase was a Supreme Court justice, an intense Federalist. He was accused of browbeating witnesses and of making intemperate speeches from the bench. A dutiful House impeached him, and the Senate called him to trial. If *he* went, it was generally agreed, Chief Justice Marshall would be next.

Burr presided with aplomb. He was at his best. The proceedings were long and colorful, attracting large crowds, and in the end Chase was found not guilty, which infuriated the President; but his worst enemies could not deny that Vice President Burr had been scrupulously fair and at all times dignified and impressive. He had covered himself with glory.

You can't eat glory. When the Senate session ended, March 4, Aaron Burr made a touching farewell speech to his associates. He was not ordinarily a spellbinder, not a man who strove for dramatic oratorical effects, but on this occasion he outdid himself. Many, perhaps most, wept. This, too, did the Vice President no good.

He was now just another man without a job—and without any money, for money was a commodity that had always slipped through his careless hands. Politically and professionally there was no place for him anywhere in the East or the South. (In both New York and New Jersey there were still warrants out for his arrest.) So he went the only way he could—west. He went over the mountains.

He was a desperate man. For all his charm, his exquisite manners, his easy laugh and his wit, he was looking for trouble. He got it.

CHAPTER

5

He had entered a world of whispers. He had always been a quiet man, reserved, sociable enough, but leery of committing himself even in private conversations. He also had a boyish delight in mystifying people, a delight he was about to indulge. Everywhere he went rumors swirled behind him like the turbulent wake of a ship—juicy, sucking, susurrant rumors. Obviously he was looking for a future, and being the sort of man he was, he would hardly be satisfied with something small, something dim. It was said of him that he was going to set up an independent republic west of the Mississippi, with himself as its permanent president (Napoleon Bonaparte only recently had proclaimed himself an emperor, and almost anything along these lines was believable); it was said of him that he was about to anticipate the expected war with Spain by invading Mexico and making himself that country's king; that he planned to raise a pitchfork army along the Tombigbee and, at the head of this, take over first West Florida and then East Florida; that he had an elaborate scheme calculated to cause Ohio, Tennessee, Kentucky, and the territories of Mississippi and Orleans, and perhaps even Georgia, to break off from the Union and declare themselves free of those effete and thieving easterners. He himself said nothing—aloud. The speeches he was called upon to make were purely conventional in their nature, and any plotting that he might have done—and he was certainly up to *something*—was strictly of the backroom, low-voiced variety.

It was also possible that he was seeking a home and a law practice in some state—Tennessee was suggested, as was Ohio—where the residents did not frown upon the shooting of Federalists and where his peculiar talents might be better appreciated. His friends assured him that if he settled down in this fashion he would have small difficulty getting elected to the national House of Representatives, which, quite likely, would make him its speaker, no minor honor. But if he was tempted by such talk he gave no sign of it.

He left Philadelphia April 10 and rode for nineteen days, until he reached Pittsburgh, a flourishing little town at the confluence of the Ohio, Allegheny, and Monongahela rivers, where he took possession of an ark he had ordered by mail.

This was a sort of raft with a house on it, measuring 60 feet long by 14 feet in beam. It had a dining room, a kitchen, and two bedrooms, and the roof could be used as a promenade. It had glass windows and a wood-burning fireplace. There was no sail, and there were no oars or thole pins. There were poles, but these were not meant for propulsion, only for pushing the craft out to midstream whenever a curve in this sinuous river caused it to nudge a bank.

In this, accompanied only by a secretary, a few friends, and the faithful Peter, Burr floated down the Ohio, making, sometimes, as much as seven knots, tying up to sleep any place he fancied.

May 3 he was in Wheeling, and May 5, Marietta, at the

HARMAN BLENNERHASSETT.

MRS. BLENNERHASSETT.

mouth of the Muskingum, where he examined the curious Indian burial mounds and conferred with local officials.

A few miles from there, downriver, he came to Blennerhassett Island, of which, and of the owner of which, he had heard much.

Harman Blennerhassett was a learned Irishman of musical proclivities, the proprietor of a dwindling fortune. He had bought this island, which was three miles long and very narrow, comprising about 300 acres,[13] and on this, with the aid of a handful of servants, he had built a large sprawling house and a beautiful series of gardens, and he was presently engaged in experimenting—with no remarkable success—in the growth of hemp. He had been there eight years.

Blennerhassett had a little money left. He was reputed to possess a great sense of wonder and a gay credulity, and, according to Dudley Woodbridge, a former business partner, he had "every kind of sense but common sense." He was so nearsighted that at ten paces he could not tell a man from a horse, and he had a loose jaw: he loved to talk, talk. Such a man would be worth seeing. Aaron Burr always needed money, and he was very persuasive.

As it happened, Blennerhassett was not home; he had gone to Cincinnati on business, so Burr did not have himself announced. Instead, he landed and strolled around for a little while, admiring the gardens, until Mrs. Blennerhassett, a vivacious if not particularly attractive woman, saw him and invited him to stay for dinner, which he did. It was the beginning of a beautiful friendship.

Cincinnati, a city of 1,500 population, was the next stop, where Burr spent six days. During much of that time he was in close conference with John Smith, a land speculator, Baptist preacher, storekeeper, army contractor, and recently elected United States senator; and Jonathan Dayton, a friend of Princeton days, who until a short time earlier had been United States senator from New Jersey,[14] and who, like so many others, was out West to look at land. Whatever their talk was about, there was no rattle of arms connected with it, and when Burr resumed his voyage he still had only a small party and no guns at all except such few as might be carried for potshotting. For all the flurry of rumors that he was about to raise a filibustering army, he flapped no flags and beat no recruitment drums. He was out, this time, only for a good look around.

He was warmly received in Louisville, and from there he went by horse to Frankfort, where he was the guest of Senator John Brown. He was in Lexington May 22, 23, and 24, and once again a big fuss was made about him. From Lexington he rode to Nashville, where he stayed four days at The Hermitage, his host being that lank, lantern-jawed major general of the Tennessee militia, Andrew Jackson.

Jackson lent him an open boat, and he was rowed 220 miles down the Cumberland to the Ohio River again, where his ark was waiting for him.

From the mouth of the Cumberland it was only sixteen miles to Fort Massac, an army post, and here he was greeted by General James Wilkinson, with whom he had missed connections in Pittsburgh. These two, who had met originally in the Philadelphia home of Charles Biddle, were eager to meet again. They had a lot to talk about.

Burr was at Fort Massac for four days, the sixth through the tenth of June, and the talks, of course, were secret. However, anything that touched James Wilkinson was bound to be defiled.

The man has gone down in history as a fool, and this is unfortunate, for he was not. It is true that he was fat, ruddy, and fond of food and drink, and that he ranted so much

GENERAL JAMES WILKINSON.

about his honor that a hearer could be sure he had none. It is true that he wore gaudy uniforms, and strutted, and made speeches and wrote letters that were soggy with pomposity. But behind the cap-and-bells there was a shrewd, hard-reasoning brain—and no conscience at all. The general knew everybody, and he could grab an honor or a dollar at almost any distance. He might *look* like Falstaff, but he could behave like a rattlesnake. After a Revolutionary War career marked largely by tumult and intrigue, he had resigned from the army with the rank of colonel, and had gone west to speculate in land and, in New Orleans, to deal in tobacco. Failing in both those pursuits, he went back into the service, and after a while, the proper men having died, he became a brigadier general and the commanding officer of the whole United States Army. This was the United States Army at its lowest hour, for Jefferson the President was a determined pacifist; nevertheless, Wilkinson *was* its commander, and as such was a very big wheel, indeed, in the West, where most of the army was stationed.

While still a civilian he had been prominent in the movement that became known as the Spanish Conspiracy, a movement aimed at alienating the western states from those of the east in order to make the Union a smaller threat to the Spanish possessions. It is probable that he did this either for money or for special tobacco trading rights in New Orleans, or both. It was at this time that he got on the Spanish payroll, where he was officially listed as Agent 13, getting $2,000 a year. Naturally, he did not advertise this fact. It is possible, though unlikely, that Aaron Burr was unaware of it.

Whatever it was that Burr was planning, it would need the cooperation or at least the blessing of the Commander-in-Chief, who, parenthetically, liked to call himself the Washington of the West.

Wilkinson fitted him out with a truly splendiferous barge, all flags and bright paint, and lent him a bodyguard of ten privates and a sergeant. The party was beginning to take on grandeur.

It was seven days to Natchez, where, as everywhere, he was wildly acclaimed; and on June 25, sixty-seven days after he had left Philadelphia, he stepped ashore at New Orleans with all the air of a conquering hero.

CHAPTER

6

It was a fixed American belief that any land or municipality that was swept under the protective mantle of United States democracy should consider itself blessed and should from that time onward never cease to give forth prayers of thanks to God for having so lifted it. The residents of New Orleans did not feel that way. Of the sundry flip-flops the oldest among them could remember—French to Spanish, later Spanish to French again for a mere three weeks, and now French to American—the last seemed the worst.

The "ancient Louisianians," as the Creoles liked to be called, did not have a high opinion of Americans, whom they esteemed Huns, Vandals, barbarians. And, for the most part, the Americans whom they had seen *were*.

The New Orleans that Colonel Burr visited in the summer of 1805 was a big busy city, its population of about 9,000 being augmented from time to time by seamen from the hundreds of vessels that tied up there in the course of a year, and by the men who handled the keelboats from the north. The deep-sea mariners were something of a problem, as sailors always have been in all ports, but they were of many nationalities and fitted well into this highly cosmopolitan atmosphere. They might have been unpolished, but at least they were human.

It was not so with the keelboat men, and, to the Creoles, all Americans were keelboat men. *They* were shaggy and surly beyond belief, boisterous drunkards, sots who stank. They would sell their goods—pelts or flour or bear oil or whatnot, and sometimes the boat as well—and then, paid in cash, go on a glorious spree. In time, of course, they would run out of money and have to start home, but there were fresh keelboats coming down the river all the time.

The original oppressive law under which the colony was to be governed had been broadened a bit. The city could now have its own aldermen and was to be allowed, also, a nonvoting delegate to Congress. But the Creoles, hurt, took little advantage of this, which they regarded as a dubious gift at best, and at worst an insult.

Fortunately the Americans did not flood into New Orleans immediately after the Purchase, but came only in driblets. Most of them were merchants and were highly successful, which did not endear them to the "ancient Louisianians," who thus had to work harder to stay alive.

There were not many incidents but there was a great deal of hard feeling, and officials like Governor Claiborne and General Wilkinson as well as visitors like Aaron Burr spent a great deal of time trying to determine whether, in the event of a war with Spain or an internal uprising, these disgruntled Creoles would be loyal to a government they had never asked for.

Burr, to be sure, was no keelboat man. Not only was he *simpatico*, he could speak French. His famous charm had never before been used to such effect. He was wined and dined and fussed over, a lion.

He was delighted with the sultry, flamboyant city. He wrote to Theodosia that if only he could have her with him, together with her son, Aaron Burr Alston, he would like to live there for the rest of his life. Did he think it possible that she might some day come to him, to be the hostess of his royal court in this, his royal capital? Did he picture his grandson-namesake as an heir apparent, a prince? Whatever form his activities eventually took, they were almost certain to center on this river port. Even if he invaded Mexico to the full, all the way, right up to and into the halls of Montezuma, which he might well occupy as a palace, New Orleans would be his jumping-off place, his principal base for supplies, his recruitment center. To any one of the schemes he nourished it was indispensable.

Whether or not the Creoles would have stood aside in the event of a breaking-up of the Union, whether or not they would have remained nonparticipants in an attack upon Mexico, most assuredly the American residents of the Crescent City were in favor of such an attack. There existed there a Mexican Association of some three hundred members (many of them prominent and rich), formed for the purpose of gathering information that might be useful to an invader—official or otherwise—of Mexico. In the three weeks he spent in New Orleans, Burr saw a great deal of the Mexican Association. He was the guest of an old New York friend who had started a flourishing law practice in the South, Edward Livingston, himself a member, but his most valued letter of introduction, given him by General Wilkinson, was to David Clark, a merchant of Irish antecedents, who made much of him. Clark might or might not have been a member of the Mexican Association, but he was heart and soul in favor of it. He had recently been elected delegate to Congress from the new territory. He had agents in Mexico, a country he was about to visit in person, and he assured Colonel Burr, as did so many others, that the place was ripe for revolt. Bitterly as the Creoles hated the Americans, the Americans seethed with an even more virulent hatred for the dons—not the Mexicans themselves but their Spanish masters, who were always called that. The land would burst into a revolution of its own accord very soon, Burr was told. All that was needed was a leader.

They clamored for what they called a war of liberation.

They might have been right. *This* was the hour. Had Burr struck then, had he been in a position to lead a filibustering force at least into the Mexican province of Texas, he might well have scored a victory, changing the course of history. The Louisiana Purchase convention had been vague about the boundaries of that vast territory, and already there were sharp differences of opinion between the United States and Spain, with both sides edgy. President Jefferson might abhor war and work in every way against it, but nine out of ten Americans of the time—and not just in New Orleans, but all over the nation—believed that a war with Spain was inevitable and that it would come soon.

Aaron Burr undoubtedly believed this as well, but there was nothing that he could do about it—for the present. He needed more money. He always needed more money.

He had started to try to raise funds while still Vice President. He had sent a personal friend, an Englishman, to interview William Pitt on the subject, for he believed that Pitt would see the advantage of having the American Union split, and he followed this move by approaching the British ambassador, Anthony Merry, in Washington. Merry was enthusiastic, and recommended a policy of cooperation to Whitehall. Burr had estimated that about $110,000 would be enough for a beginning, provided two or three British war vessels were sent to patrol the mouths of the Mississippi. How he planned to blockade the Mississippi without precipitating a war between Great Britain and the United States he did not say.

He also had the effrontery to approach the Spanish ambassador on the same errand. This personage, Don Carlos Martinez Yrujo, Marqués de Casa, an elegant, redheaded jumpingjack of a man, was not as naïve as Merry. He believed Burr to be a British agent, and he shied away from him, though very politely.

Another possible source of funds was the banking group that was openly backing the efforts of Francesco de Miranda to outfit a military expedition against the Spanish government of Venezuela. However, these bankers were centered in New York City, and that was not a healthful neighborhood for Aaron Burr.

From New Orleans, Burr returned to Natchez, where there was another week of celebrations, and from there, mounted, and attended by a single servant, he went by the 450-mile, bandit-infested Natchez Trace to Nashville. He was again the guest of Jackson and of Senator Smith, and again he acted like a man running for office. He backtracked to St. Louis, where Wilkinson was, and they had another long, secret conversation. The only *immediate* and *visible* effect of this talk was that Wilkinson sent a small scouting party under Lieutenant Zebulon Montgomery Pike to map a trail to Santa Fe, an expedition that had no effect upon Burr's plans, though it did result in the discovery of Pike's Peak.[15]

Burr went up the Ohio, visiting Cincinnati and Blennerhassett Island—his previous trip in reverse. Early in December he was back in Philadelphia, where he spent a busy but quiet winter.

William Pitt died in January, though, as it turned out,

he had previously turned thumbs down on the Burr appeal for funds anyway. The new government, headed by Fox, would have nothing to do with the scheme. Yrujo was more coy than ever. Burr was introduced to Miranda, whom he liked personally but whom he regarded as a rival filibusterer. The moneyed men like Samuel G. Ogden and William S. Smith, Miranda's chief backers, had committed themselves too deeply to have much cash to spare; and once again Burr, though he got something, was disappointed.

The only bright spot in the picture was the behavior of the Spaniards in the southwest, where they had crossed the Sabine, a river that by tacit agreement was to serve as the boundary between Louisiana and Mexico until more definite arrangements could be made. This might be interpreted as an act of war, and certainly Wilkinson—though he was not on the spot, being still in St. Louis—could turn it into war, legitimately or otherwise, any time he so wished.

It was not until August that Colonel Burr, now heading a small party, left Philadelphia for the west—"never to return" was the way he put it. To prove this, he took Theodosia with him.

CHAPTER

7

THERE WAS IN Washington that winter a much-pointed-out figure in a sombrero, a red silk sash wrapped around his waist. He was impetuous, impatient. His name was William Eaton, and he insisted upon being addressed as "General." Aaron Burr was to meet him there, to Burr's lasting regret. Burr may even have sought him out, for Eaton was a professional adventurer, a man distinctly on the make, the Hero of Derne.

A Connecticut Yankee born in 1764, at seventeen he had run away from home to join the Continental Army in the Revolution. He was a sergeant at nineteen, a tall blue-eyed lad, handsome in a harsh way. After he got out of the army at the end of the war he somehow managed to enroll at Dartmouth, teaching school on the side. He was graduated with a bachelor of arts degree at twenty-seven. He opened a school in Windsor, Vermont, at the same time becoming clerk to the Vermont legislature. In 1792, through political pull, he got a captain's commission in the United States Army. He did not last long. He was court-martialed on a charge of misappropriating government property, and, though the findings of the court-martial were never officially verified, he was again out of a job. But he knew the right people, and in 1797 he was sent as United States consul to Tunis.

There were three North African nabobs in those days who were, to all intents and purposes, pirates. They were the Dey of Algiers, the Bey of Tunis, and the Bashaw of Tripoli, fat, bearded blackguards who stole from the Mediterranean commerce of sundry European nations—or, rather, forbore so to steal for a set, yearly price. The nations might splutter—and they did—but they came across. The United States also did. American envoys to France, when Talleyrand hinted at a bribe, cried: "Millions for defense but not one cent for tribute!" but in Africa, along the Barbary Coast, America paid. These were regular, written agreements, international treaties, though the word "tribute" was never used in them.

The Bashaw of Tripoli thought that he was not getting his share—not as much as his "cousins" in Algiers and Tunis. He was a particularly unsavory potentate named Yusuf Karamanli, called, sometimes, Yusuf the Bloody, who, in order to ascend to the sacred sofa, had murdered one of his older brothers; he would have murdered the other if that nimble person had not skipped the country just in time. Yusuf, then, in 1801, demanded a big rise in his blackmail payments from America; and America paused, meaning only to haggle; but Yusuf, in a fit of rage, declared war. This of course would give him the chance to prey upon American shipping no matter what the previous financial arrangements had been.

The *un*murdered brother of Yusuf had taken refuge in Tunis, where the Bey supported him, if somewhat shabbily, doubtless thinking that he might come in handy some time. This was Sidi Mahomet Karamanli, better known as Hamet, a wan figure of a man who felt very sorry for himself. Consul

Eaton saw that this man, if he could be persuaded to lead a revolt against his younger brother's already shaky sofa, might serve to bring about a quick and inexpensive ending to the war. Without any authority, Eaton sought out Hamet and began to argue with him.

It was a naval war, and Eaton had said some sharp things about the way the United States Navy was running it. Nevertheless, he was able to get certain guarded half-promises of cooperation from the captains, and he went back to work on Prince Hamet.

Yusuf the Bloody heard of these negotiations, and he spoke to the Bey of Tunis, perhaps accompanying the request with a bribe—they could work well together, these ruffians—and the Bey of Tunis cut off Hamet's income; whereupon the rightful heir, for the first time being obliged to earn his living, decamped to Egypt, where he enlisted in the Mamelukes, an outfit that promptly thereafter mutinied.

All of this complicated William Eaton's task, but he went, undaunted, to Egypt—first Alexandria, then Rosetta, at last Cairo—where he managed to arrange to get Hamet quietly out of the Mamelukes.

Between them, after great exertions, they assembled, March 3, 1805, at the Arab's Tower on the desert just west of Alexandria, what surely must have been one of the most tatterdemalion armies in all history. There were 107 beasts of burden, most of them camels, singularly uncooperative creatures, and a company of rebellious Arab camel drivers to care for them. Hamet had a personal bodyguard of aristocrats mixed with waterfront cutthroats, numbering ninety. There was a troop of Arab horsemen led by two temperamental sheiks. There were thirty-eight Greek foot soldiers, though just how they got there nobody seemed to know. There were twenty-five cannoneers. There were also six United States

Marines under a corporal, a United States Navy midshipman named Peck, and a lieutenant named O'Bannon. There was a British surgeon, Farquhar. There was also a courier-interpreter-military engineer-general factotum known at that time as Eugene Leitensdorfer, though at various periods in the past he had been called Gervasio Santuari, Carl Hossando, Padre Anselmo, and Murat Aga, an unquenchable soldier of fortune who had also served as a monk, a dervish, and the proprietor of a coffee house and of a theatre,[16] and who could speak just about every known language.

When they left the Arab's Tower March 8 they numbered about 500, of whom about 100 were Christians—or, at any rate, non-Moslems. However, this number varied wildly as men deserted and then came back again, and as informal enlistments were made in villages and oases along the line.

For more than six weeks this rabble stumbled 500 miles through some of the grimmest countryside in all this world.[17] April 15 they fetched up at the Bay of Bomba, where a navy cruiser was supposed to be waiting for them with supplies. They were half starved, largely mutinous, and burning with thirst, for while the march had been for the most part within sight of the sea, it had afforded almost no fresh water.

The cruiser was not there. Nothing was there.

It was a near thing for a while. The Arabs (the term is a generic one, for in fact all sorts of nationalities were represented) swore that they would quit for good—next morning. They were fingering their muskets meaningfully so that when the Christians had retreated to the nearby hills, they could not be sure that they would survive the night. For this reason they kept their camp fires burning.

In the morning the fires had been spotted from far out at sea, not one but two Navy vessels, *Aggus* and *Hornet*, each loaded with supplies, sailed into Bomba Bay. That made all the difference. The desertion threateners decided not to desert after all, and those who had already done so came down from the hills. Everybody ate and drank a great deal, and the remaining forty-odd miles to Derne, the only mentionable town between Alexandria and the capital, Tripoli, were a romp.

Yusuf was sending a huge relieving army. The defenders of Derne, about equal in numbers to the attackers—about 1,000 now—knew this, and it made them even less inclined to fight. Hamet's men also knew it, and they were eager to take the town right away, so as to gain the protection of its walls. There were three navy cruisers in the offing now, and they peppered the citadel at will, softening up the garrison. With gusto, Hamet's and Eaton's men struck, and in a matter of little more than minutes the Stars and Stripes was fluttering, for the first time, over a foreign fort. Losses had been trifling. Eaton himself was wounded, but only slightly.

The ending of the story is a sad one. Reinforced from the sea, the invaders gallantly fought off Yusuf's relieving column, but as they braced themselves to start a march on the Capital, word came to Consul Eaton from the navy that all hostilities must cease. An agreement had been signed with the Bashaw, giving in to virtually all of his demands, and Hamet was to be ditched.

They sneaked away in the dark of the night—rowboats, muffled oarlocks—the non-Moslem officers, the Greeks, the Marines, the cannoneers, Hamet, Eaton himself, Eugene Leitensdorfer-Santuari-Hossondo, and whichever other Christians there might have been—for it seemed certain that these would be massacred when the others learned what had happened—and that was the shameful finish of it.

"General" Eaton was made much of when he returned to America. He was cheered in the streets, dinners were given for him, toasts were drunk, and Boston renamed a street

Derne. But he was broke. The Commonwealth of Massachusetts, to be sure, awarded him 10,000 acres of Maine, and he was able to sell about half of that at 50 cents an acre, but this was not much for a man of his drinking habits, and he went to Washington to try to collect his expenses: he claimed to have spent more than $20,000 out of his own pocket. Congress did talk for a while about striking a medal in his honor, but this fell through. Eaton went on pulling strings; he was still, after all, the hero of Derne.

This was the reason that he turned down Aaron Burr's offer of a place in the forthcoming expedition to the southwest. No. He would get that money, somehow. He would think of a way. He did.

It is likely that Burr wanted Eaton because of his name rather than because of any military abilities the man might be supposed to have. Burr was never unaware of his own military capacity. His record in the Revolution had been brilliant, and despite his youth, the only reason he did not rise to a rank higher than that of colonel was that ill health forced an early resignation. At the time of the near war with France, a brigadiership became available, and Burr promptly applied for this; but Commander-in-Chief Washington preferred, as more reliable, Alexander Hamilton.

Burr also approached a couple of other popular heroes of the day, both of them naval. Commodore Thomas Truxtun, Burr's host at Perth Amboy after the duel, had covered himself with glory again and again, and he was surely the most capable mariner in the land; but he was too much a strong-navy man to suit President Jefferson, and when, in the course of a long-range controversy, the doughty Truxtun had seemed to be offering his resignation, Jefferson instantly accepted, though Truxtun protested that he had never meant any such thing. It was a low trick, for it knocked Truxtun's whole life

THOMAS TRUXTON.

out from under him: he was fifty, and had been at sea since his early teens. He might be expected to be bitter, as indeed he was, and prepared to heed the siren song of a western adventure, which, as it turned out, he did not.

Burr then tried dashing young Captain Stephen Decatur, whose burning of the lost frigate *Philadelphia* in Tripoli harbor under the guns of the fort had been one of the few memorable deeds in a war in which the country as a whole could take little pride; but Decatur, too, was not interested.

Still, there were some choice spirits who would take part in the enterprise.

There was Comfort Tyler, of Herkimer, New York, a young man of promise, once a member of the Assembly, who had fallen upon evil days and had been arrested for vagrancy in New York City, where Burr rescued him, bailed him out, and set him on his feet again. Tyler, eternally grateful to his patron, was now employed in western New York, where he had many connections, recruiting and buying supplies for the expedition.

There was Colonel Julien de Pestre, cool, experienced— he had served in both the French and British armies and his title was clear—who acted as Burr's chief of staff.

There was young Samuel Swartwout, son of the United States marshal in New York, a lad who before this had acted as Burr's secretary and was currently engaged as a courier.

There was Dr. Justus Erich Bollman, who spoke excellent English as well as French and German, and who was of special value to Burr because of the aura of fame about him: he had been the one principally responsible for a daring attempt to rescue the Marquis de Lafayette from his Austrian prison, and Lafayette was a demigod to Americans.

And of course there was General Wilkinson. Burr and the commanding officer had corresponded for years, using a cipher in which the President was represented by a circle, the Vice President by a circle with a dot in it, the Secretary of State by a dash with dots above and below, and so forth— a cipher any child could have broken down. Wilkinson had been silent for some months, but now, early in August, he wrote. This epistle was characteristically magniloquent, and characteristically vague; but at its end, not in the cipher but in plain English, the General had written: "I am ready."

Good. Aaron Burr was ready too. He set forth from Philadelphia.

CHAPTER

8

Names would have helped, but it was money that he most needed. Colonel John Swartwout, Sam's father, and a few other financial friends in the New York Burr himself must needs avoid had helped some, but most of these were low in funds as an aftermath of the Miranda expedition. The Spanish and British ambassadors, on whom he had counted so heavily, turned up never a cent. His son-in-law, Joseph Alston, was reputed to be one of the richest men in the South, but his wealth was all in land and after two droughts he had almost no cash to spare. Alston could, however, and did, raise money on his land, and this he turned over to Theodosia's persuasive parent. Even so, Aaron Burr, when he set forth, probably had less than $50,000 with him, not a tenth of what he had estimated he would need for an opener.

Advance agents were ordering flour and pork by the hundreds of barrels, and Comfort Tyler and other authorized recruiters were told to offer young men $12 a month, besides their clothes and keep, for six months, and 150 acres of Louisiana territory as a bonus at the end of that time. Nothing was said about firearms. Colonel Barker of Muskingum, a few miles above Marietta on the Ohio, was put under contract to make fifteen boats, ten of them 40 feet long, five 50 feet, all with a 10-foot beam, of shallow draft, and propelled by oars. These should be capable of holding 40 to 50 men each, with their gear.

The land promised was an important part of the whole scheme. Just before the switch-around, Hector, Baron de Carondelet, the last Spanish governor of Louisiana, had granted to Filipe Neri, Baron de Bastrop, some 1,200,000 acres of rich, arable land in the northern part of the Territory of Orleans along the Washita (or Ouachita) River.[18] Neither the French take-over government nor the American government that had followed it in a few weeks had verified this grant, and its legality could be questioned. Charles Lynch, a Shelby County, Kentucky, lawyer, had got control of about three-fifths of the land. Burr on his first trip west, had bought about half of Lynch's claim for $5,000 down, in the form of a draft on George M. Ogden of New York, one of Miranda's backers, and a note for $30,000 drawn against the transplanted attorney, Edward Livingston, in New Orleans.

This claim to 400,000 acres of land nobody had ever seen was a wobbly one at best, but in a place and at a time when men thought big in terms of acreage, it was impressive.

Not only did it lend an air of responsibility to the expedition, it also served to supply whatever 150-acre grants might be handed out to volunteers. More, if by any chance war with Spain had not broken out by the time Burr and his men got down there, if something had held up General Wilkinson, they could always fall back upon this de Bastrop tract, pretending that it was what they had come for in fact, and *all* they had come for. They could settle there, build an idyllic civilization (Burr was an incorrigible optimist, and his imagination soared at the thought of this new Eden), and *be* there, ready, near the Texas border, when war *did* break out.

Pittsburgh was the first important stop, a center of the gathering supplies, and the party stayed there several days. On August 22, Burr, accompanied by Colonel de Pestre, rode out to Morganza, an estate near Cannonsburg, about fifteen miles from Pittsburgh, to call upon and dine with an old friend from Princeton days, Colonel George Morgan.

There was to be speculation, later, about the purpose of this visit. Colonel Morgan was a much older man than Aaron Burr—at Princeton they had known each other as neighbors, not as fellow students—and they could hardly have had much in common. Morgan, indeed, was teetering on the edge of senility. In late colonial days he had invested heavily in one of those enormous amorphous deals in land on the far side of the mountains—in this case both north and south of the Ohio River. He was not alone in this deal, for other reputable men had invested, but he was alone in the persistence with which he kept crying for his money long after the British colonial authorities, the Continental Congress, and now the federal government at Washington, had refused to validate the deal. It had always been a risky matter though not a shady one. The others took their losses and turned to something else, but Colonel Morgan had fought on, only recently, it would seem, having given up hope, so that now he was more interested in raising grapes at Morganza than in pushing his claims to the vast acreage. Nevertheless, the fight had been a famous one while it lasted, and Burr would have known about it. Burr *could* have believed that he was calling on an embittered old man who might cock an attentive ear to any plan that proposed a separation of the western from the eastern states. Or, again, he could have made the visit in the hope of enlisting the martial services of the colonel's two sons, Thomas and

John, New Jersey militiamen of considerable experience, who were currently staying with their father. This would account for his taking along De Pestre, his own military expert.

He made no recruits, nor did he get any loan or encouragement, but for such a reticent man he seemed to have talked a great deal. Next day old Colonel Morgan began to worry about that conversation. It sounded to him, as it had sounded to his sons, that Colonel Burr was actually proposing to split the Union. He would not have been the first to make such a suggestion. Certain New England Federalists were pressing it even at that moment, and west of the mountains it had become almost a commonplace. Jefferson himself, at least the pre-Presidential Jefferson, had declared his belief that the western territories had every right to break away from the East whenever they elected to do so. But this had been before the Louisiana Purchase. If all the land between the Alleghenies and the Father of Waters dropped away, what would happen to that princely Purchase?

Colonel Morgan fretted and fussed about this. He took into his confidence a couple of friends, men as old as he, and they too fussed. They advised him to write to the President, with whom he was personally acquainted; and this at last he did.

He did not make himself very clear. He insisted that it was not so much *what* Colonel Burr had said as the *way* in in which he had said it. Burr had *implied*, Colonel Morgan implied, that he was working out a separation plot; he hadn't actually *said* that.

Burr, Morgan remembered, had inquired as to the local militia situation, how many men in that vicinity could be called to arms on how short a notice, and how many had been active in the late Whiskey Rebellion.

He might, of course, have been asking those questions

only for the sake of politeness, thinking that the subject was the one that most interested his own companion, Colonel de Pestre, as well as the younger Morgans.

It has also been put forward that Burr might have had too much to drink that night. Nobody who knew him would have advanced this theory. Good company always, he was anything but a tippler, and his drinking was purely formal.

At any rate, President Jefferson received the letter, and read it, and filed it away without comment; while Aaron Burr, knowing nothing of all this, rode on.

It was at Blennerhassett Island, reached now for the third time—but the first time when the owner was in residence— that the Great Conspiracy was to be based.

CHAPTER

9

THE EBULLIENT Irishman fell in love with Aaron Burr,
These two had corresponded, but until this time had not met.
Burr had hinted darkly, in a letter to Blennerhassett, that his
grand plan—whatever it was—might not be put into effect
until December, "if ever." When he met the man face to
face, he knew that he could be more outspoken. Blennerhassett was credulity personified. He would swallow anything.
Very soon he, and his lady as well, were prattling to the help
and to casual acquaintances about King Aaron I of Mexico
and Princess Theodosia and Crown Prince Aaron Alston, for
they were bedazzled by the prospect that had been opened
before them.

Burr's friends would assure you that he never told a lie
—never, that is, *deliberately, knowingly*, lied. This could be.
There was nothing furtive about Burr, who considered himself a man of honor, and whose open manner and easy, frank-
seeming speech would appear to bear out this assumption.
Yet if he did not actually utter falsehoods for the purpose of
deceiving, it cannot be denied that he knew how to shade

the truth. He knew how to say one thing in such a way as to make his hearer think that he meant something quite different.

Thus, if called upon to do so, he could always swear that he had made no sort of deal with any foreign nation, while tactfully refraining from mentioning that for almost two years he had been *trying* to make such a deal.

Thus, he would protest that he owned no arms or other military supplies, and at the same time forget to add that he was planning to buy or to seize some, and also that his recruits were expected to carry their own weapons, which he, Burr, did not *own*.

Thus, on this trip west, as on that of the previous year, he everywhere gave the impression that there were greater forces behind him than met the eye; that, though he was not supposed to say this in so many words, his hearers could readily deduce that official Washington approved of his plans, for how otherwise could he have ventured this far? In truth, this was easy to believe. After all, the man had missed the Presidency by only one vote. He knew everyone, and had been everywhere. Nobody but a fool would suppose that the powers-that-be in Washington would permit such a personage to go traipsing around the West talking mysteriously of a descent upon Mexico unless the said powers-that-be fully approved of such a descent, which might well strengthen their hand. As for the talk about a western secession from the Union, that would be no calamity. The average person west of the mountains, one who knew anything about public opinion there, must have assumed that if a separate government were set up, a government of Americans, at New Orleans, controlling the mouths of the Mississippi, all of the states and territories in the West would in a little while—not right away but within a few years—take up with that government. This would be only natural, geography being what it was, and trade what *it* was. No expedition in specially built boats would be needed to bring about such a movement.

Harman Blennerhassett probably had been a separatist long before Burr came to his island. At a time when Burr no longer was there, but undoubtedly inspired by his late presence, the proprietor wrote four articles for the *Ohio Gazette* of Marietta, in which he accused the mercantile East of exploiting the predominately agricultural West, and favored a separation—perhaps not an immediate separation, but a separation just the same. Burr must have known about these articles before their publication. They were signed "Querist," but nobody questioned who had written them.

The island was all astir. Boats came and went as recruiters visited neighbors. Enlistees were assigned to quarters in the outbuildings. Corn was roasted in kilns, and ground. Water bottles were filled. Yet there was nothing martial about these arrangements. There were no bugle calls, no parades, nothing to cause apprehension among those who lived nearby, who nevertheless *were* apprehensive.

As for Mrs. Blennerhassett, she was delighted. In all the years they had lived on this island, they had not had a chance to entertain distinguished guests; and now they had under their roof not only a former Vice President but also his incomparable daughter, the lovely, languishing, and altogether charming Theodosia Alston, besides many other, more local, notables, who came and went importantly.

The air was buoyant with expectancy. Men walked around as though the ground beneath their feet was pneumatic.

Comfort Tyler came out from New York with a handful of recruits. Blennerhassett dropped down the river a little to stir things up in another neighborhood. Colonel de Pestre went to St. Louis to talk a while with General Wilkinson, and then went east to New York and Philadelphia, trying to raise more money. Burr himself scuttled here and there, confirming old friendships, conferring with supporters such as General Adair and General Jackson, men who were keen for the adventure and who would certainly join up as soon as war broke out.

Andrew Jackson even issued an order to all Tennessee militiamen—he was the commanding officer—to stand by for action. He sent a copy of that order to President Jefferson, who must have been startled by it. Burr sent another copy to William Henry Harrison, governor of Indiana Territory, with a note suggesting that he issue a similar order; but Harrison held his hand.

Jackson, like so many other westerners, was interested in many business projects at the same time, including, always, land speculation. Burr offered him a contract to build five large shallow-draft boats on the Cumberland River, suitable for ferrying troops down to the Ohio; and Jackson, though he had never before done anything like this, accepted with alacrity. Burr paid him $3,500 in cash—in Kentucky state bank notes, part of a $25,000 loan he had just raised from the Kentucky Insurance Company.

October 6, Burr left Frankfort and joined Blennerhassett and the Alstons at Lexington, which for a short while was to serve as a sort of central headquarters for the expedition.

Things seemed too good to be true.

Those wild rumors, glittering and popping, as iridescent as soapbubbles, but poisonous, still pursued him. Blennerhassett Island was a part of Wood County, Virginia,[19] and the folks in those parts got worried at the goings-on and held an impromptu mass meeting at which it was agreed that the militiamen of the county should hold themselves in readiness to investigate in force if such action seemed advisable.

Hearing of this, Mrs. Blennerhassett sent out two servants to warn her husband and Aaron Burr against an immediate return to the island, something neither of them had planned anyway.

The one who carried this message to Burr, a gardener named Taylor, seems to have been something of a halfwit. "The people there will shoot you if you come back," he solemnly said. Burr only smiled.

To learn where Burr was in the first place, Taylor had applied to John Smith, the United States senator-elect, in his Cincinnati store; and Smith, who had contracted for some supplies for Burr and was troubled about the spate of rumors, sent a message with Taylor, asking specifically if Burr planned any secession movement. Nothing could have been more candid, it would seem, than Aaron Burr's reply:

"If there exists any design to separate the Western from the Eastern States, I am totally ignorant of it. I never harbored or expressed any such intention to any one, nor did any person ever intimate such design to me."

The rumors varied, but all of them included a horde of troops. Two thousand was the smallest number of men mentioned, and estimates ran as high as 30,000. In truth there were fewer than fifty men quartered on Blennerhassett Island, and they were not hoodlums but young men of good family brought out not by avarice or orneriness but by love of adventure. They were quiet and well behaved, and most of them were unarmed. All the same, the Wood County militia did not see fit to descend *en masse* upon Blennerhassett Island until these lads had dropped downriver, making for Lexington.

Somebody had warned Mrs. Blennerhassett just in time, and under cover of darkness she slipped away with the last few servants, clinging to what books and art objects she could carry.

The militiamen won a victory that was bloodless—but it was wine-stained. They smashed furniture, they muddied the rugs and the carpeting, and they broke into the cellar, a famous one, after which they had a grand old time getting drunk. They found no military supplies.

Others besides Colonel Morgan were warning the President that affairs in the West were about to come to a boil. One of these, one of the most persistent, was Joseph Hamilton Daveiss, the young, handsome, and hotheaded United States attorney for the Lexington district.[20] He was a Federalist, left over, and most of those he denounced were Democrats, so Jefferson was cool to his suggestions. This did not faze Daveiss. November 3 he went into action.

He asked Federal Judge Harry Innes, in Frankfort, for a warrant to arrest Burr on charges of conspiring to invade Mexico and cause a separation of the eastern and western states. A few days later Judge Innes ruled against this, declaring that it was a grand jury matter, whereupon Daveiss asked that a grand jury be empaneled to hear the charges, and this was done. Daveiss, however, had to ask for a postponement in order to summon a certain witness, and it was not until December 2 that the jury actually heard the charges.

Burr had been in Lexington, about to start back to Marietta, when he heard of this court action. He changed his plans and rode to Frankfort, where he put up as a house guest of Judge Innes, and where he hired a lawyer, a twenty-nine-year-old man named Henry Clay, who had just been appointed to the United States Senate.

The retaining of Clay was something of a triumph, lending Burr respectability, for the young man who was about to go to Washington for the first time was known for his unalterable integrity. Before he took the case, he insisted that Burr assure him that he was planning no revolution, no disruption of the Union, which Burr did, even putting it into writing.

The circumstance that the last time Daveiss and Clay had faced one another was on the field of honor helped to pack the courtroom. That duel had not been fought, but only because at the last moment friends of both parties had physically intervened, insisting upon a settlement. There still was no love lost between them.

Burr, as always, handled himself with quiet dignity, never raising his voice, but the crowd got its money's worth when Daveiss asked for permission to question witnesses personally before the grand jury, and Clay sprang to his feet, shouting objections. After this, the two had at it with hammer and tongs in the orotund oratory of the day.

Clay won. The motion was denied. The grand jury not only refused to hand down a true bill but actually issued a statement praising Aaron Burr for his behavior and his patriotism. The statement was printed as a handbill and widely distributed by Burr's friends, who that very night gave their hero a bang-up victory dinner in the local tavern.

Once again, everything looked all right. But everything wasn't.

10

Exactly when it was that General Wilkinson decided to rat on his partner is a question that will never be answered.

It may have been when he learned of the death of William Pitt and the taking over of the British government by Charles Fox and his "cabinet of many talents." This would mean the end of all hope for British financial support. Money never meant much to the airy Aaron Burr, but it did to James Wilkinson. Pitt had died January 23, 1806, but the General did not hear about this until April or May, when he was in St. Louis.

It may have been when he got a long cipher letter from Burr, October 8, telling him that the expedition was already under way.

undated
see p. 152
footnote

Or it could have been almost any time between those two events.

Wilkinson, whose appointment as governor of the great, new, and almost unpopulated District of Louisiana had barely squeaked through the Senate, was not well liked in St. Louis, where his high-handed methods were opposed by Samuel

Hammond, whom the General in a letter to President Jefferson characterized as "a hackneyed scoundrel," and by Return Jonathan Meigs, a survivor of Arnold's march to Quebec, to Wilkinson "a poor, pimping, hypocritical Yankee." It could be that his fear of the machinations of these men in his own absence was what caused him to dally so long in the river town after Secretary of War Dearborn had ordered him to go to the southwestern border and repel the advancing Spaniards, who had already crossed the Sabine. Or it could be that, with Burr in mind, the General simply wanted to see which way the cat would jump when it was let out of the bag. It is hard to trace the workings of that labyrinthine mind.

Whatever the reason, he loitered for months, avoiding the explosive situation to the south, and when at last he did lumber forth, he was in no hurry. Once he had crossed the thirty-eighth parallel, he was in the Territory of Orleans, where Claiborne, whom he despised—and whose job he had tried to get—was the civilian governor. Wilkinson himself, however, was the military chief of both territories, as well as of the Territory of Mississippi, east of the big river.

He reinforced the camp at Natchitoches, near the center of the Territory of Orleans and about fifty miles from the Sabine River. September 23 he wrote to the Spanish commander, Cordero, telling him to get back across that river.

Cordero's reply was curt. He said he had no authority to order a retreat.

The expectancy of war tingled in the air.

It was at this time, in the camp at Natchitoches, that Wilkinson was handed one of the two copies of Burr's letter. Young Sam Swartwout gave him this, having traveled with it by land. A few days later Dr. Bollman, who had come by sea, handed him a duplicate.

At the same time there was delivered to the General a

note from Jonathan Dayton, Burr's closest associate, warning him that he was about to be superseded as commander of the army. This was a jolt. Dayton was a former United States senator and would know what he was talking about in matters political. A failure in business, the General badly needed his command in the West. It was patent that he had to do something to make himself seem indispensable. He must become a hero. He had always wanted to be, anyway.

Burr's letter [21] alarmed Wilkinson, or he pretended that it did. He took almost two weeks to ponder it and to touch it up, and then he wrote to President Jefferson of his "discovery" that "a numerous and powerful association, extending from New York through the Western states to the territories bordering on the Mississippi, has been formed with the design to levy and rendezvous eight or ten thousand men in New Orleans." He did not name Burr; he did not need to. He wrote that martial law should be proclaimed. At the same time he asked for a raise in pay, complaining that he couldn't live on what he got.

Even while he did this, he had a friend and aide, Walter Burling, in Mexico, trying to get more than 100,000 pesos out of the Spanish government for past favors the General claimed he had performed. Burling did not succeed in this mission, which ostensibly was for the purpose of buying army mules. The Spaniards knew their Agent No. 13 too well. The trip was not an utter failure, however. Wilkinson put in a bill for $1,200 for Burling's expenses, and the Treasury, after President Jefferson had personally endorsed it, paid it.

The field commander of the Spanish force east of the Sabine, Herrera, in an unexpected burst of common sense, announced that he would withdraw to the other side of that river, and he did so.

Though Wilkinson was in correspondence with Vincente

Folch, the Spanish governor of West Florida, as well as with the government at Mexico City, there is no reason to believe that he had been notified of this move. It was simply a stroke of luck, of which he was quick to take advantage.

He struck an on-the-spot agreement with the Spaniards that both banks of the Sabine should be sacrosanct until such time as the higher powers of both nations could frame a formal pact. This, known as the Neutral Ground Treaty, was signed, on the field, on November 5.

The deal went directly against Wilkinson's orders, for the government at Washington, foiled so far in every attempt to buy or annex either of the Floridas, still was contending that the Louisiana Purchase included all the land between the Sabine and the Rio Grande—in other words, the whole province of Texas—whereas the Neutral Ground Treaty virtually recognized the Sabine to be the southwestern boundary of the United States. This was to cause much trouble later; indeed, it was to bring about a war; but immediately it was a windfall for the General. He could now pose as a farseeing statesman who had averted a war—as in truth he had, though through no merit of his own—and he had as a perfect excuse the threat of the Burr expedition. Above all, New Orleans must be protected! He needed every man he could muster!

Also, his Spanish pension would continue now. If there *had* been a war, the General would have been out that $2,000 a year.

The General might drag his feet when obeying an order he did not like, but in a corner he could be as quick as a cat.

In the plan that had sprung full-formed into his brain it would be necessary to paint his coconspirator, Aaron Burr, in the blackest colors obtainable, make him the deepest-dyed of all possible villains. The scummier the scoundrel Burr, the brighter the savior Wilkinson: it was as simple as that.

The Deliverer waxed strident. He wrote to various colonels, begging them to be prepared to do or die right away. He sent one to New Orleans with orders to put that city into a state of defense as soon as possible, the enemy being, he inferred, almost in sight. He wrote to the President that he could trust no one, that he still did not know (this was a lie) who was the leader of this strange but terrible march upon the city, that there were several men who had sworn to assassinate him; and he added that while he did not fear death on the battlefield whilst struggling for his country, he *did* dislike the prospect of being stabbed in the back.

Chin up, in fact both of them up, he went to Natchitoches and gathered reinforcements. November 25, breathing fire, his sword arattle at his side, he entered New Orleans at the head of these men to inaugurate what came to be known there as the Wilkinson Reign of Terror.

For the ten or twelve days that Sam Swartwout had remained in the camp at Natchitoches, Wilkinson treated him with every courtesy, though all the while striving to worm out of him the story of Burr's plans. Now suddenly, with no apparent provocation, Wilkinson ordered Swartwout's arrest, together with that of his young companion, Peter V. Ogden, and, without even the pretense of a trial, hustled them off to a United States Navy frigate for shipment, in irons, to Baltimore.

He called a mass meeting of patriots, whom he harangued fiercely and at length, all but bringing about a panic. Either he was frightened (which seems unlikely, for he was not a physical coward) or he was putting on a show.

He demanded of the civil governor, Claiborne, that he declare martial law, and he demanded the same thing of that weak reed the territorial legislature, in both cases getting a frightened refusal. Wilkinson nevertheless acted as though martial law *had* been proclaimed. He ordered a curfew. He accepted volunteers, both American and Creole, who paraded in the Place d'Armes by day and by night patrolled the streets. He stationed a force of soldiers about sixty miles up the river with orders to stop and to thoroughly search every craft that came down. No vessel of any sort was to be allowed to leave the port of New Orleans, whether upstream or down.

In none of these moves did he make any pretense of authorization or legality. He was acting in an emergency, to save the city from ravagement by the rabble that was about to descend upon it, he said, and he could not, as an honorable soldier, stand idly by and wait for orders from faraway Washington.

He sent off a dispatch to Jamaica, to the admiral in charge of the British Navy in Caribbean waters, warning him to watch out for freebooters from New York or Philadelphia bound for Vera Cruz or for the mouths of the Mississippi —a message that must have mystified the admiral.

He seized Dr. Bollman, once again without a warrant, and, denying him any sort of trial, shipped him off to Baltimore in a navy vessel.

One James Alexander, a local lawyer, got a writ of habeas corpus for the release of Ogden, but Ogden was promptly re-arrested, and Alexander was arrested as well, Wilkinson proclaiming that he personally had suspended the habeas corpus statute. He even arrested Judge Workman, who had issued the writ, that he, Wilkinson, flouted; but he was obliged to let Workman go.

When General John Adair arrived in New Orleans from Kentucky, he repaired to Madame Nourage's boarding house, where, weary after the long trip, he wrote a letter to Governor Claiborne making known his arrival and asking the governor to pass on his respects to General Wilkinson, upon whom he would call in person later. Then he sat down to enjoy one of the house's celebrated dinners. But Adair was closely connected with Aaron Burr and at one time had had dealings with Wilkinson himself, dealings the General would not like to hear made public at this stage of the game. So, more than one hundred United States soldiers in uniform surrounded Madame Nourage's establishment and carried out the poor General (he was in his sixties) before he could even finish his meal. He was hidden in a tent some miles outside of the city for the rest of the day, and after dark he was sneaked aboard a frigate for the customary treatment.

Meanwhile, where was that horrendous horde? When did the balloon go up?

CHAPTER

11

THOMAS JEFFERSON, though calm, had not been as unaware of the doings in the West as some of his correspondents
appeared to think.

He called a cabinet meeting October 22, at which the
matter was discussed, the President revealing the letters he
had received. It was decided to write to the governors of
Ohio, Mississippi, Indiana, and Orleans, and the district attorneys of Kentucky, Louisiana, and Tennessee, admonishing
them to keep Burr "strictly" watched and to have him seized
the moment he committed any "overt act." This sounded
weak; but after all, they had no evidence, only hearsay.

Two days later the cabinet met again and ordered Edward Preble and Decatur to go to New Orleans and take
command of whatever naval force was stationed there, for
the purpose of preventing any possible outbreak in the city. At
the same time, one John Graham was sent to Kentucky with
orders to pick up Burr's trail and follow it closely, and to
arrest the man "if he has made himself liable."

The very next day, however, a large batch of mail came in from the land beyond the mountains, and there was in it not a hint of any lawless activity along the Ohio or the Mississippi, so that the cabinet members, a mite sheepishly, decided to countermand all their previous orders, except that Graham was still to be sent out.

Graham went—a quiet man, as befitted his mission. He interviewed Blennerhassett, who babbled. He interviewed others, gathering information. Aaron Burr never even knew he was back there.

It would be some time before Graham's reports began to arrive, and those in Washington relaxed, supposing that the crisis was over. Then, with the impact of a bombshell, there came to the White House the letter General Wilkinson had written October 21 from the camp at Natchitoches, the letter in which he made known his "discovery" of the secret, sinister plot to crush and plunder New Orleans and to rip the West away from the East. In the same mail was a letter from Governor Claiborne saying much the same thing. Claiborne only had his information from Wilkinson, but the officials in Washington did not know this; and after all, Claiborne *was* the governor, and he was, clearly, a frightened man.

This arrived November 25, the very day on which, a thousand miles away, James Wilkinson was riding into New Orleans.

Radical action was called for. The President issued a proclamation.

Wilkinson's shrill warning had not included the name of Aaron Burr, and neither had that of Claiborne. The letter framed a little earlier to be sent to the various governors and federal distict attorneys held Burr's name clearly enough, but this letter had been countermanded, and in any event it was meant to be strictly confidential.

The proclamation [22] did not spell out the name of the leader. Avoiding details, it warned all and sundry that certain persons were "conspiring & confederating together to begin & set on foot, provide & prepare the means for a military expedition or enterprise against the dominions of Spain," and enjoined "all faithful citizens who have been led to participate in the sd unlawful enterprises without due knolege or consideration to withdraw from the same without delay." Civil and military officers of the federal government as well as of the various states and territories were cautioned to be vigilant.

That did it. That sealed the doom of the Great Conspiracy. A few days later, in his sixth State-of-the-Union message, the President scarcely mentioned the accumulation of military forces and stores in the West for the apparent purpose of invading Mexico, and did not mention Burr at all; but the proclamation was to have a powerful effect in the West, where it was widely distributed. The sight of the Great Seal of the United States was a sobering douche for many who previously had been inclined to consider Burr's expedition as something of a sporting event. It was no longer that. It was serious now.

All unknowing and as sunny as ever, Colonel Burr rode into Nashville. General Jackson was not at home, but his lady, Rachel, was strangely cool, and the Colonel, not invited to stay at The Hermitage, took rooms in a local inn. Moreover, the work was not finished. Only two of the five boats ordered were ready to put into the water, and his recruiting officer had signed up only ten men of the seventy-five expected. Soon Andrew Jackson himself appeared, and he too was cold, for he had been given to understand that Burr's real purpose was to split the Union in two. Burr, who could have charmed the birds down out of the trees, soon convinced him that the only aim of the expedition was an in-

vasion of Mexico, a project of which Jackson heartily approved, and that the government in Washington was secretly back of the whole business. Jackson, thawed, apologized about the boats; but Burr said that he could not wait. Jackson paid back out of the original $3,500 the amount he had not spent—$1,725.62—and Burr, with these scanty reinforcements, dropped down the Cumberland for a junction with Blennerhassett and the main body.

This meeting was held on Cumberland Island, where the two rivers meet. Burr harangued the combined forces. If he was disappointed, he didn't show it. Serene as always, his fine dark eyes shining, he explained that he had intended to make a public statement about the aim of the expedition in this place and at this time, but now he thought that this would have to wait a little while. (The truth is, he feared that there was a spy in the force.)

It was a part of Burr's policy to move the men downriver in small batches, so as not to cause too much talk. There was talk anyway. Stories were told of huge barges filled to the gunwales with cannons and with foreign-looking, fierce-looking mercenaries. Five hundred would be a small figure for one of these reported passages. In fact, Burr had fewer than one hundred men on Cumberland Island, and probably the figure was nearer sixty.

He had eleven boats: ten for men, one for supplies. None of the former was as much as half full.

He was undismayed. He would recruit as they went; and, anyway, the reinforcements from Blennerhassett Island would be along soon. If all the boats he had ordered, at Nashville, on the Muskingum, and other points, were delivered in due time, he could easily have accommodated 1,500 men; and the extent of his food supplies purchased in advance and waiting, espe-

BURR'S TROOPS GOING DOWN THE OHIO RIVER.

cially at Natchez, indicate that this was about the number he expected to have before he got down to business.

But—John Graham had persuaded the Governor of Ohio and the authorities of Wood County, Virginia, to call out their unmannerly militiamen. The fifteen boats built and building on the Muskingum near Marietta were confiscated. Young men who kept appearing in small groups at Blennerhassett Island, were being sent back east. The first ones were arrested, but nobody could think of anything to charge them with, so they were released. None, however, got through.

It took the adventurers two days to get down to Fort Massac. They had sent a man ahead to announce their coming, and the commanding officer, Captain Daniel Bissell, was delighted to see them. Two days later Bissell was to get an order to arrest Burr on sight if he was engaged in any suspicious activity; but they were all gone by that time. Bissell even lent them the services of a sergeant, one Jacob Dunbough, to whom he issued a twenty-day leave.

As 1806 was turning into 1807, this curious aquatic caravan turned from the Ohio River into the muddy, muddy Mississippi.

January 4 they tied up under the Chickasaw Bluffs,[23] where there was an army post in charge of Lieutenant Jacob Jackson, son of an old friend of Burr's. They spent the whole day there, and by the time it was finished, Burr had talked Jackson into agreeing to resign his commission and, as a captain under Burr, to raise a company. Burr gave him $150 cash for expenses. Young Jackson, like Bissell, had not yet heard of the Presidential proclamation.

True, at Chickasaw Bluffs Burr learned of Wilkinson's activities—the signing of the Neutral Ground Treaty and the falling back into New Orleans. The first was a disappointment but no disaster: Burr assumed that it had been unavoidable and had been done on direct orders from Washington. The second suited his purposes perfectly. He did not doubt that Wilkinson was in New Orleans in order to prevent Governor Claiborne from calling out the militia,[24] and that the gates of the city would be thrown open at the approach of his little force. Lieutenant Jackson assumed the same.

January 10, a little less than a week later—it was a Saturday—they approached the settlement of Bayou Pierre, about thirty miles above Natchez, in the Mississippi Territory. Burr went ahead in a small fast keelboat. He was looking forward to a visit with his friend Judge Peter Bryan Bruin, a man who loved his liquor.

He met the judge, all right; and the judge showed him a copy of the *Mississippi Gazette* of Natchez, dated January 6, that contained President Jefferson's proclamation, a decipherment of Burr's long letter to Wilkinson, and news that a warrant had been issued for Burr's arrest.

The game was up.

12

GOVERNOR FOLCH, as soon as he heard about President Jefferson's proclamation, moved 300 Spanish troops from Pensacola and Mobile to Baton Rouge, on the Mississippi, the westernmost edge of West Florida. This was ominous. Baton Rouge, it was widely believed, would be the first town upon which the enormous forces under Aaron Burr would pounce.

General Wilkinson and Governor Claiborne, in New Orleans, wrote to the acting governor of the Territory of Mississippi that they understood that Aaron Burr "has taken post within the territory over which you preside," and that they "cannot but express our solicitude, lest his pretensions to innocence . . . may be partially successful."

"We rely with confidence on your exertions to seize the arch-conspirator," they went on, "and having done so, permit us to suggest to your consideration the expediency of placing him without delay on board one of our armed vessels in the river, with an order to the officers to descend with him to this city." [25]

In other words, they wanted to get their hands on Burr.

They might have saved themselves the trouble. The acting governor, who was also secretary of the territory (the governor, George Williams, was visiting kin in North Carolina), was a young man by the name of Cowles Meade, and he was at no loss as to what to do. As soon as he got a copy of the President's proclamation, he applied to Claiborne—but in vain—for a loan of additional arms and ammunition. He deplored the fact that General Wilkinson had recently caused Fort Adams to be stripped, thereby depriving the Territory of Mississippi of its one military arsenal. He prorogued the territorial legislature, so that its members who held militia positions, as virtually all of them did—along a thinly settled frontier every man could count—might be free to go about those more imperative duties. He sent a force of men upriver to stop and examine any suspicious vessels that came down. December 23 he issued a proclamation of warning to all citizens of the territory. On Christmas Day he ordered his aide, William B. Shields, to call out the four regiments of militia.

Cowles Meade was not to be caught napping.

A couple of days before Burr arrived at Bayou Pierre in person, he sent a letter ahead to the acting governor, protesting that he and his men had no thought of opposing in any way the federal or the territorial governments, and expressing the hope that they would be heard before they were opposed. When Meade learned, on the morning of January 11, that Burr had spent the previous night in the home of Judge Bruin, he sent a squad to nab him. Burr had already gone back to Bayou Pierre, a spot upon which 375 members of the Second and Fourth regiments were converging, but he had left an open letter to the inhabitants of the Territory of Mississippi saying again that he was willing to explain his intentions to the civil authorities.

The word "civil" should be stressed. The moment he saw

that his letter to Wilkinson had been given to the press, Burr knew that he must keep out of the General's hands. The General, should he capture his one-time partner, could and almost undoubtedly would take advantage of the hysteria he had done so much to incite. Acting under his own declaration of martial law, he could and probably would haul Burr before a drumhead court and, pleading the emergency, have him shot.

The military chief of an outlying district like that, so far from the capital, *months* from any written directive, had extraordinary powers.

While the Colonel conveniently absented himself, some of his officers that afternoon at Bayou Pierre explained the situation to the men. The Mississippi militia were known to be making for this point, but the men were assured that they had done nothing wrong, and nothing of which the federal government would not approve. If it came to a showdown, would they fight for the Colonel? They voted that they would.

Yet it was considered safer, under cover of the night, to cross the river to Thompson's Bayou on the Louisiana side, and even there the few firearms were passed out and sentries were posted.

Burr was now in an all-but-impossible position. He could not back into his Ouachita River lands without first descending the Mississippi to the mouth of the Red River, some fifty miles below in a straight line, considerably more than that as the river wound; and this part of the Mississippi might well be patrolled by federal gunboats. He could not go north without risk of running into a party of reinforcements (for he still believed that some such party was on the way) and this might precipitate a panic; besides, in Ohio and Kentucky, and perhaps Tennessee as well, the hue and cry would have been raised against him. To go south was unthinkable: that way lay

Wilkinson. To stay where he was would mean Wilkinson too, in time. His best bet, as he saw it, was to cross the river back into the Mississippi Territory; but could he be sure that the trigger-happy militiamen over there would not bring about a brawl, which would be fatal to all concerned?

On the morning of January 13, Major Wooldridge, with thirty-five men, the first of the militia up from Natchez, arrived at the mouth of Cole's Creek on the Mississippi side. They were going to be uncomfortable, for they had come without tents and the weather was cold and wet. Nevertheless, they encamped.

Burr sent a skiff to ask if some of the officers would not come over and have a drink with him. Wooldridge and two others took this terrible risk. They were delighted, though probably not amazed, by the graciousness with which they were received. They surely *were* amazed by the appearance and behavior of Burr's rank-and-file. They had no doubt expected scowling illiterates, men with whiskers, with daggers in their teeth. What they saw was as fine looking a lot of lads as anybody could ask.

Probably as a result of this visit, on January 16, when the whole of the Second and Fourth were unsatisfactorily settled at the mouth of Cole's Creek, two more official visitors were admitted. These were Major Shields, the acting governor's military aide, and George Poindexter, the United States attorney general for the territory.

The business was beginning to assume the aspect of a duel, with representatives bowing to one another before and after they had set forth stipulations. Indeed, a sort of cartel was drawn up, and all three men signed it.

Cowles Meade would guarantee the personal safety of Colonel Burr if the Colonel would call upon him the next morning at Thomas Calvit's house on Cole's Creek. His men would not be attacked at that time, and his property would not be damaged. In turn, Colonel Burr must guarantee that his men would remain where they were at least until he returned, and would not start any trouble.

Burr caused himself to be rowed across the river the next morning, and a company of dragoons met him at the mouth of Cole's Creek and escorted him to the Calvit home, where he met Cowles Meade.

They talked for a couple of hours, but they did not get far. All Burr asked was a chance to explain himself, but the acting governor was skeptical. Meade already had sent for his chief, Williams, who was undoubtedly on his way, and Meade was disinclined to make any ironbound promise in the meanwhile.

It was agreed that Burr would surrender to the territorial authorities at Washington, a little town near Natchez that served as the capital, and that Mississippi militia officers would be permitted to search his vessels for military supplies. Further than that Meade would not go.

The next fortnight passed smoothly enough, even pleasantly, except for the miserable militiamen encamped at the mouth of Cole's Creek. (There had been four inches of snow in one night, far more than the oldest resident could remember, and they were still without tents.) Burr gave himself up in Washington, Mississippi, and was held over in $10,000 bail. A couple of friends—he had friends everywhere—easily produced the bail. Out in that remote place there were not many distinguished and worldly visitors, and the Colonel was made much of in Washington and in nearby Natchez—dinners, dances, balls, everything. Here he was perfectly at home. His men crossed the river again and tied up just above Natchez on the Mississippi side, where they began to fraternize with the natives, who, much to their own astonishment, found these Yankees, these banditti, to be right good company.

Burr even had time for a romance, reputedly, with a maiden called Madeline Price; but then, he always had time for things like that.

The persistent John Graham caught up with him here and applied for an interview. This Burr refused because—as Graham reported to his chief, Secretary of State Madison—he was committed to the court.

His manner remained genial, his manners exquisite, but he was nagged by two thoughts: (1) which way should he dart when once he was freed? (2) could he survive the attentions of Wilkinson until that time? The second was no idle fear. It was not founded upon mad rumors, of which there were many, but on knowledge of General Wilkinson. The General had committed himself. It was Burr's head or his. What would prevent him, with his resources, from sending a kidnapping squad after Colonel Burr, men who would not be in uniform, who would be spurred by the thought of a big cash prize, and who might just accidentally kill their victim as they seized him? [26] Every day Aaron Burr spent in and around Washington, Mississippi, was a day of danger.

February 2 he was brought to trial.

13

It was the territorial Supreme Court, and there were two judges—Peter Bryan Bruin, who liked Burr, and Thomas Rodney, who didn't.

District Attorney Poindexter moved to have the case transferred to a lower court, for the Supreme Court, he said, was wholly a court of appeal. He added that he did not see any cause for an indictment.

Judge Rodney said no, and he called for the formation of a grand jury. This was done, and after two days of taking depositions—the prosecution had had two weeks in which to prepare its case—the jury not only refused to return a true bill but issued a statement deploring the calling out of the militia, the treatment of Aaron Burr, and the outrageous out-of-hand arrests in neighboring Orleans Territory: "and they do seriously regret that so much cause should be given to the enemies of our glorious Constitution, to rejoice in such measures being adopted in a neighboring Territory, and if sanctioned by the Executive of our country, must sap the vitals of our political existence, and crumble this glorious fabric into the dust."

That was Wednesday afternoon, February 4. Judge Rodney was furious. The grand jury was dismissed, chuckling.

Burr moved that he be released from his recognizance. A bail bond had been posted on the assumption that he would stand trial and be acquitted; but he had not been tried, had not even been indicted, and there was no charge against him. Judge Bruin would have let his friend, and house guest, go. But not Judge Rodney. Judge Rodney held Burr to his recognizance, ordering him to report to the court every day.

This was an unheard-of procedure and in the long run no doubt could have been proved unconstitutional. But there was no time for a long run. Captain Hook and his kidnap squad already were on the scene, putting up in a house just outside of Natchez, which was only about six miles from Washington, and they might snatch the "arch-conspirator" at any minute. More, Governor Williams was back on the job, and it was common knowledge that he planned to turn Burr over to the Orleans territorial authorities as soon as extradition proceedings could be instituted—and as soon as the court released its prisoner.

Burr talked things over with his friends. There seemed to be nothing else to do but run for his life. He addressed his men, telling them that they could shift for themselves. He regretted that he could not pay them, for the New York banks had refused to honor his money orders and he had no cash, but they might sell the equipment if they wished, and they might go to the lands along the Ouachita, if they could get there.

Then he disappeared. It was the day after the end of the trial.

Governor Williams, who had resolutely refused to consider Burr as anything but a fugitive from justice, offered a reward of $2,000 for his recapture.

There was a stir. All of the members of the filibustering party were taken out of their boats and placed under arrest, but nobody seemed to know what to do with them, and so, with a few exceptions—Harman Blennerhassett, Comfort Tyler, Davis Floyd—they were soon released. A few of them found their way back east, but most of them settled down right there where they were, in a land and among a people they liked. None of them made their way to the Ouachita River lands. The boats and the remaining supplies were sold, and the money divided evenly. The boats, being of unusually strong construction, brought seventy-five dollars each, two to three times as much as boats of that size usually brought there.

It was February 18, very late, in Washington County [27] on the road that led toward Pensacola, and a gigantic young lawyer, Nicholas Perkins, was lolling in the doorway of his office shack: he was a registrar of lands. He heard two horsemen coming from the west.

This was odd. Here was a thinly populated country district down near the West Florida boundary, and who would be riding so late at night?

Soon they came into sight. The first passed without a word, but the second reined before Perkins. He was tiny—to the registrar he must have appeared almost a midget—and he was dressed in homespun, with a floppy white felt hat on his head. Under that wide-brimmed hat it was difficult to make out the man's facial features, but Perkins was conscious at least of a fine pair of luminous dark eyes. He noticed that it was an elegant, well-polished boot that came out of the bottom of the rude pantaloons, and certainly too the voice in which this traveller asked the way to Major John Hinson's house was not the voice of a country bumpkin.

Perkins told him, pointing. But he warned him that the creek he would have to cross would be dangerous in the darkness, for it was swollen. They'd had an exceptionally wet winter in those parts.

The little man thanked him and rode on.

Perkins got to thinking about it. Could this possibly be the notorious Aaron Burr, for whose capture the governor of the territory a couple of weeks ago had posted a $2,000 reward? He could be heading for Pensacola, where a British warship rode at anchor. Or he could be aiming to rouse the settlers along the Alabama and Tombigbee rivers, inciting them to rebel against the Spaniards in West Florida. Major Hinson, though well known and respected in Washington County, was of uncertain political affiliations.

Perkins awakened the sheriff, Theodore Brightwell, and together they rode out to Major Hinson's. The sheriff went in. Perkins remained in the woods, watching.

They seemed to be having a very pleasant little supper party in there, in the kitchen. He could hear laughter from time to time. After a long while the candles were whuffed out; but the sheriff did not emerge, and evidently he was staying the night.

Shivering, for it was wet, Perkins rode back to Manna-hubba Bluff, where from a friend he borrowed a canoe and a Negro who paddled him down the river to Fort Stoddert. The small garrison at the fort was in charge of Lieutenant Edmund Pendleton Gaines,[28] who listened to Perkins' story and decided to investigate. They took along a sergeant and three privates.

At about nine o'clock they came upon two riders. One was the little gentleman with the fine eyes who had asked Perkins the way to the Hinson house. The other was Sheriff Brightwell, who, fascinated by the little gentleman, was guiding him to the road to Pensacola. (The other horseman, who turned out to be Major Robert Ashley of New Orleans, had

THE ARREST OF AARON BURR.

started west from the Hinson house earlier that morning.)

Burr put up an argument, making sure that Lieutenant Gaines knew the penalty for false arrest, but Gaines was firm, and they rode back to Fort Stoddert, minus the sheriff.

Once again the Colonel was to prove an embarrassing prisoner. This was not because he was balky. On the contrary, he was all amiability and cooperation. He lent and borrowed books, and discussed them wittily. Gaines's brother, a dealer with the Choctaws, lay ill of a fever, and the prisoner, who turned out to have had a certain amount of medical training, nursed him tirelessly. He played chess with Gaines's wife. Women in the neighborhood fell in love with him only from glimpses. One of them named a baby after him.

Lieutenant Gaines was worried because, in the first place, he was waiting for orders as to what to do with this man, and, in the second place, he feared that a mob might try to free him. The people in that vicinity were a rough lot, and they would have welcomed a personage of military background who could lead them against the dons.

At last the order came—not from Wilkinson, certainly. Colonel Burr was to be taken to Washington, D.C., which was almost nine hundred miles away, much of it through wilderness.

Nicholas Perkins, who, after all, would get most of the reward money, was commissioned to lead the party, and Gaines gave him eight privates. They started March 5. It rained most of the time. They had only one tent, which the prisoner was permitted to use, but the men were forbidden to converse with him, for Perkins was properly fearful of the Burr charm.

Despite the weather and the ruggedness of the terrain, especially during the first week, the prisoner never uttered a word of complaint. He still wore his countryman's costume.

There was only one touch of unpleasantness, and that was in the town of Chester, South Carolina, near the North Carolina line. It was the largest and most civilized place they had yet come upon, and as they were about to ride past some men standing before a tavern, Aaron Burr sprang off his horse and cried out that he was being held illegally by the army and that he demanded to be turned over to the civil authorities. Perkins ordered him back on his horse. Burr refused. Perkins dismounted, picked him up as though he had been a naughty boy, and slammed him back into his saddle.

After that they hired a gig, and the curtains were drawn when they went through towns.

At Fredericksburg, Virginia, there came a change in their orders. They should take their prisoner not to Washington but to Richmond. A stagecoach was sent for them.

They arrived in Richmond, after dark, on the twenty-sixth of March, having made the trip in three weeks, covering a little better than forty miles a day. They went directly to the Eagle Tavern, a brick structure a whole city block in extent—the south side of Main Street between Twelfth and Thirteenth streets—and almost directly opposite the Capitol, the building in which there was soon to be staged the greatest criminal trial in the history of the United States.

CHAPTER

14

THE STAGE had been well set. Richmond was a city of about five thousand, perhaps half of them Negro. It was new, as Virginia settlements went, but not *raw*-new. Unlike its predecessor, the "toy capital" of Williamsburg, it had a design; it was not chancy; instead, it had been laid out as though with a grille, its streets parallel, meeting one another at right angles, and its blocks square. This was most unusual. Philadelphia, the largest city in the country, had been laid out according to plan, and so had Washington, D.C., which, however, still was a mud hole; but for the rest, American cities were haphazard, offhand, their avenues little more than cow paths, their parks nonexistent.

Richmond, like Rome, was built on seven hills, and upon the largest of these was the Capitol, a classic Greek building designed by Thomas Jefferson himself. The sides of this hill were scarified by gullies and piles of rock. Across the way was another architectural wonder, the square fieldstone Golden Eagle tavern. Here was no ordinary hostelry. It was the best one in town, possibly the best in the country, a prodigy of elegance.

It was to the Golden Eagle that Aaron Burr was taken. To enter it, he had to pass under a sign that already was famous—an eight-by-five-foot white wooden sign on which was depicted a singularly fierce yellow eagle, the wings widespread, the eyes lit with an accipitrine gleam. This was the work of a promising young painter named Thomas Sully, who had been paid fifty dollars for it.

Richmond had been picked for the trial because the government decided to prosecute on the grounds that an overt act of treason had been committed when forces were assembled on Blennerhassett Island, a part of Virginia. The Supreme Court of the United States was not then exclusively an appeal body. Its members went out on the road from time to time. Richmond happened to be in the bailiwick of the chief justice, John Marshall, and it was he who would hear the case against Burr.

Marshall was to be as much on trial as Burr, and he knew it. The President, with impeachment proceedings in mind, was watching him carefully, waiting for him to make a misstep.

These two, Thomas Jefferson and John Marshall, were as much alike and at the same time as startlingly different as had been Alexander Hamilton and Aaron Burr, and they hated one another quite as virulently. Both were Virginians, sons of pioneers. They were, in fact, third cousins once removed, each being descended from the famous couple William Randolph and Mary Isham, sometimes known as the Adam and Eve of Virginia. Jefferson was excessively shy, introverted; but Marshall was an easy mixer, though by no means effusive. Neither pretended to be brilliant. Each took his time. Marshall was dark, Jefferson sandy, but both were long and rangy of build, and each was a sloppy dresser. In politics they were natural enemies, holding diametrically op-

CHIEF JUSTICE JOHN MARSHALL.

posite views as to how the government should be made up and how it should operate. Jefferson of course was a Democrat-Republican. Marshall was a Federalist.

Burr was kept at the tavern under a sort of house arrest for the weekend, but he was at least allowed lawyers and writing materials, so that he could tell Theodosia about it. He learned, there, what had been going on in the world while he made that three-week trip through the wilderness, skirting towns, being permitted to talk to no one, and never seeing a newspaper.

Wilkinson's various victims, shipped east in chains, had been released on writs of habeas corpus, there being no grounds on which to hold them. In the cases of James Alexander, Peter V. Ogden, and General Adair, this had been done promptly after they came ashore. The case of Samuel

Swartwout and Dr. Bollman, the couriers, took a little longer and involved an angry courtroom battle; but the thing had been done, and the men were free.

The President's prestige was at stake. He had first been elected to the Presidency in 1800, tying with Aaron Burr, winning at last by one vote in the House of Representatives after thirty-five ballots had been taken; but his second victory, his reelection, had been clear cut, so that now he believed that the great majority of his countrymen were behind him. He had publicly branded Aaron Burr guilty: his "guilt is placed beyond question," he had written in a message to Congress January 22, and he had underlined the words.[29] The Supreme Court decision freeing Bollman and Swartwout alarmed him. If those Federalist judges could bring in verdicts like that, might it not be conceivable that the traitor Burr would be acquitted on some legal technicality? Burr should certainly not be permitted to go free, anyway, even on bail, even for just a little while. The President instructed his personal representative in the Senate, William Branch Giles of Virginia, to bring up in secret session a law that would suspend the issuance of habeas corpus writs in cases where treason is charged. Giles did this promptly and pushed such a bill through, with only one senator voting against it. The Senate then took the unprecedented step of sending this to the House of Representatives, with a message recommending that the House do the same, and immediately. The House, however, was not to be pushed around. It considered the matter in an open debate and decided against it. The right of habeas corpus still stood.

All of this Aaron Burr learned as he languished behind the sign of the Golden Eagle, trying on new clothes.

Monday morning there came a distinguished visitor, the Chief Justice himself, John Marshall. He did not go so far as to call upon Burr in Burr's own chambers, but he did send for him to come to one of the public rooms downstairs, and there the first hearing, the arraignment, was held.

The United States District Attorney, George Hay, had objected to this tactic. It was the Democrats' plan to take advantage of the wave of anti-Burr feeling that was sweeping the country, and for this reason they wanted the trial in all its phases to be as public as possible. Hay consented to the session at the Eagle only with the understanding that if any arguments were to be heard, they would be heard in the courthouse on the hill. Perkins was asked to give his own account of the arrest and delivery, and with gusto complied.

Burr himself then spoke, briefly, without passion. He was never an arm-waver, a shouter. Verbal fireworks were not for him. He specifically denied that his running away was any sign of guilt. He had run, he said, only after careful conference with sundry friends, who agreed with him that his life was in danger. He pointed out that he had been seized by the military without a warrant or any apparent cause, and that he had been held incommunicado for almost a month, though no charge had been made against him. He demanded his release.

The Justice listened politely, and then passed on to other things.

The Attorney General of the United States, Caesar A. Rodney (a son of the Judge Rodney in Mississippi who did not like Aaron Burr) said a few words of no consequence; after which he went back to Washington, 134 miles away, where he was to remain for the rest of this long trial, in which he took no part, unless he did so behind the scenes.

Hay, a capable enough public servant but a plodder, outclassed here, asked that the defendant be committed for trial on two charges: high misdemeanor, inasmuch as he had plotted a war against Spain, and treason, inasmuch as he had plotted a war against the United States of America.

Both sides conceded that this would involve discussion, so Justice Marshall adjourned court until ten o'clock the following morning in the courthouse. He released Burr until that time in $2,500 bail.

The crowd, next morning, was importunate. It looked as if everybody in Richmond was there, with a few out-of-towners as well. Not only the courtroom but every other part of the building churned with the curious, and the grounds outside were jammed.

Burr was half an hour late, which caused rumors to spread that he had skipped his bail. When he appeared, flawlessly dressed in black silk, his hair powdered and tied in a queue, he apologized. He had misunderstood, thinking that the Chief Justice had said eleven, not ten.

The Justice accepted the apology, and after a motion by Hay, decreed that in order to allow as many of the public as possible to witness the judicial procedure, the court would adjourn to the Hall of Delegates in the Capitol, the biggest chamber south of Washington. The Virginia legislature was not then in session.

The Hall of Delegates was a huge, sprawling, unattractive room with lugubrious, pewlike seats. Its principal decorations were square unpainted boxes filled with sand (the delegates, especially those from upstate, were fond of their chewing tobacco).

The government based its case for commitment on three papers: depositions from Wilkinson and "General" Eaton, and Burr's alleged letter to Wilkinson.

Eaton already was in Richmond, and Wilkinson was known to be on the way; they could be called later. Their depositions, in any event, were hardly crushing. Wilkinson's was

a welter of polysyllabic froth. Eaton's was an informal history of conversations he said he had had with Burr while the
two of them lived in the same Washington boarding house,
conversations in which the usually careful Colonel had talked
of assassinating the President and stealing the whole American navy as a mere preliminary to setting up an independent
empire in the southwest. This deposition, wobbly enough in
itself—Eaton had no writings to back it—was rendered even
weaker by the public knowledge that Eaton had kept these
conversations quiet for more than half a year, though in that
time he had once asked the President to appoint Burr to an
ambassador's post in Europe. There was, too, the additional
fact that as soon as he *had* come forward with the stunning
news, the United States government had paid him $10,000 of
the money he said it owed him—money he had been trying
for almost two years to collect. The hero of Derne was not
convincing.

The letter Bollman and Swartwout had carried was
something else again.

The original was never produced, only Wilkinson's own
decipherment, and there were those who believed that there
was no original, for the letter sounded to them much more
Wilkinson-y than Burr-y. Certainly Bollman and Swartwout
had delivered *something*, but Wilkinson could have destroyed
this. The paper that was read in court at the arraignment
was sufficiently damning, telling as it did of the collection
of men and money, and of the thought of seizing Baton Rouge
(which, however, was Spanish property then), and it might
be thought significant that at no time did Burr himself either
identify it or deny that he had written it.

The letter, however, could hardly be construed to show
any intention of making war upon the United States of America.

After hearing arguments for two days, the Chief Justice announced that he would write his decision that night, and he read it, gravely, slowly, the next morning, April 1, in court.

It pointed out that treason was the only crime defined in the United States Constitution, all others being the duty of Congress to define. It quoted Blackstone, of course. It failed to find enough evidence in what the government had so far presented to justify holding the defendant over on a charge of treason. That could wait. If the defendant had indeed assembled or started to assemble an aggressive army on Blennerhassett Island five months ago, the United States government surely would have little difficulty proving this.

But the Chief Justice *did* find enough evidence to justify holding the defendant over for trial in the United States Circuit Court May 22 on the charge of high misdemeanor. Unlike treason, this was a bailable offense. Marshall thought that $10,000 bail would be "about right," and he interrogated contending counsel. Hay insisted that this particular prisoner could easily raise $100,000, whereas the prisoner himself protested that he was by no means sure that he could raise even $10,000. He did so, however, and at three o'clock that afternoon he became a free man—for at least a few weeks.

The first round had gone to the defense.

Jefferson was furious.

15

THE EARLY AMERICANS were a contentious lot, always suing one another for something, so that lawyers loomed large among them. Any man with average intelligence and a modicum of education could become a lawyer in a few months, or even weeks, and a great many of them did. The courtroom was not so much a goal as a passageway. The law was a door that might lead to almost anything, and the ambitious turned to it as naturally as in medieval times they had turned to the Church.

Robin Hood, Hereward the Wake, Fulk FitzWarin, the Black Douglas, all had been left behind; but a people needs its folk heroes, and in colonial America, and in the first days of the Republic, lawyers obligingly supplied that need.

Soothsayers, toreadors, gun slingers, preachers—all have been worshipped by a supple-spined populace. Our ancestors adored the orator—which is practically to say the lawyer, since so much of the lawyer's business *was* oratory. If a man could mount spectacles on his nose and look wise, if he kept a few musty books in his office, if he could spout an occasional Latinism—best of all, if he could thunder Jovian platitudes—he was a demigod.

There was nothing subtle about the public's taste. It favored the orotund, the magniloquent. No rhetoric was too extravagant for it, no lungs too loud. Its thirst for bombast appeared to be unquenchable. It could listen for hours, for days, to the most fulsome of spread-eagling.

The Burr treason trial gave every promise of being the biggest outburst of oratory in the history of the country, and people began to come early, some of them from the other side of the mountains, some from New England, so that Richmond began to take on the air of a carnival. Those who could not get accommodations at the inns or in private houses, camped out in tents along the low land beside the river.

The visitors were of all kinds. There were mountaineers in linsey-woolsey and dandies in satin. What they had in common was a tingling sense of expectancy Their ears fairly quivered to hear the torrents of legal talk that would soon be undammed.

Aaron Burr himself was the center of attraction—after all, he was the one they had come to see convicted—but as a lawyer, though he was certainly one of the best in the business, he was not popular with the spectators, the audience. He was too dignified, too clear-cut, above all too brief. To these thrill-seekers, any attorney who spoke for less than three hours was downright curt.

Others were more satisfactory. Hay, the Number One man for the prosecution, was uninspired, but a hard worker and loud mouthed, quick to spring to his feet with objections, tough in a fight. On the same side was the lieutenant governor of the state, Alexander MacRae, a crusty old Scot with a fondness for interrupting addresses with a snort or with a sarcastic remark. That there was more of bad temper than

WILLIAM WIRT.

of wit in those remarks did not matter. They were usually
good for a laugh.

The darling of the government side, the sesquipedalianist
par excellence, was William Wirt, a young man decidedly
on his way up. His endurance was memorable, for he could
hold forth all afternoon without even pausing for a glass of
water. He could rant and roar, he could roll his eyes. He
could toss out great tangled bouquets of speech. *And* he was
funny. He had a merry grin, a natural humor. His appearance
went with all of these attainment, he being six feet tall, broad
shouldered, yellow haired, blue eyed. There was nobody
there who could compare with William Wirt when it came
to dramatic declamation. Each time he rose to his feet, a hush
fell upon the crowd.

Backing Burr was a formidable array of forensic talent.
There was John Wickham, by common acclaim the king of
the Richmond bar, who could always be counted upon to
land on his feet. He was alert, alive, versatile, and he was,
personally, a fine fellow. There was Edmund Randolph, at
fifty-four the oldest of them all, who was ponderous, learned,
profuse. A towering figure, he commanded respect, even awe.
He was eloquent too, in a slow, heavy way. He had family
connections, a very important asset in those parts. There was
Benjamin Botts, a wag, scarcely out of his teens, but un-
abashed at finding himself in such exalted company. He had
a quick comeback for everything, and was well liked by the
crowd. There was Charles Lee, who had been Attorney General under President Adams, a dry speaker, but, like Randolph,
the possessor of a powerful family name.

The crowd, indoors, was strictly male. A courtroom was
no place for a lady.

The hardest thing Aaron Burr had to face was the

climate of public opinion. The audience, to a man, believed him guilty. Had not the President himself so pronounced him? Burr might have had a few friends left in the West. He had almost none—none, that is, who were willing to step up and be counted—in the East. The newspapers of America were more than 90 per cent Democratic-Republican, and they could not think of harsh enough things to say against the defendant. Thomas Jefferson remained in the White House, but he was, nevertheless, directing the prosecution. Practically every night George Hay was to report to him by letter, carried by special messenger, and practically every day the President replied at length, giving advice.[30]

The Federal officials who had been sent beyond the mountains to gather up witnesses had been given a free hand and all the money they might need to spend. It was estimated that at least two hundred persons—lawyers, clerks, witnesses— swelled the temporary population of Richmond on the prosecution's side. And the most sensational witness of them all, James Wilkinson, had not yet arrived.

Burr remained imperturbable, to the outward eye. He was not a man to show emotion. With his beloved Theodosia, however, it was different. "The most indefatigable industry is used by the agents of government, and they have money at command without stint," he wrote to her May 15.[31] "If I were possessed of the same means, I could not only foil the prosecutors, but render them ridiculous and infamous. The democratic papers teem with abuse of me and my counsel, and even against the Chief Justice. Nothing is left undone or unsaid which can tend to prejudice the public mind, and produce a conviction without evidence."

He did not exaggerate. "Aaron Burr! May his treachery to his country exalt him to the scaffold, and may hemp be his escort to the republic of dust and ashes," was a popular toast of the time. It was generally thought—and said—that if Burr got off unhanged, it could only mean that there was something rotten in the Supreme Court, which had better be changed so that it was no longer supreme.

Midway between the arraignment and the start of the actual trial, the defense made a misstep that set an even higher pitch to the voices of its detractors. It was a superlatively stupid thing to do.

Richmond was a high-living town. A good cook was prized there, a good cellar sought out. One of the place's social features, a local development, was the lawyers' dinner, traditionally a stag affair of great cheer. One of the best-known and best-liked lawyers' dinner hosts was John Wickham, who had a large and lovely house in the fashionable Shockoe Hill section. It was natural enough, then, that while all hands waited for the opening of the United States Circuit Court, Wickham should entertain his distinguished client with a lawyers' dinner. It was somewhat less natural that he should ask his neighbor and good friend, Chief Justice John Marshall, to that dinner; and it was *considerably* less natural that Marshall, knowing that Burr was to be the guest of honor, would go. But it happened.

There was no evidence that Marshall and Burr had a drink together or sat near one another at the table, or even bowed to one another from afar; but they were both present, which was enough for the Democratic press.

The howl of indignation that rose was directed not so much at Aaron Burr, that fallen idol of whom almost any despicable deed might be expected, as at Chief Justice Marshall, who really should have known better. The Richmond *Enquirer* was comparatively mild when it called that dinner "a wanton insult he might have spared his country." Other papers went much further.

Marshall, who, like Burr, did not believe in answering his enemies, said nothing.

So stood the situation when at last there came the long-awaited May 22.

16

THE DIFFICULTY of finding unprejudiced jurors—indeed, the impossibility of it—rose right away. The first order of business was to pick a jury of sixteen out of the panel of twenty-four supplied in advance, and Aaron Burr was on his feet promptly with a technical objection. Some slight changes had been made in the panel, perhaps because of last-minute dropouts, and the defense had not been properly notified of this.

A lawyers' argument began right away, but it lasted only a little over an hour, and was ended when the Chief Justice ruled in favor of Burr. This was a minor victory.

Burr then asked for the right to challenge "for favor," and this was granted him, as was the custom. The panel members he objected to were William Branch Giles and Wilson Cary Nicholas.

Giles was majority leader of the United States Senate, and it was he who, on Jefferson's orders, had made the try at getting the right of habeas corpus suspended, an act unashamedly aimed at Aaron Burr, as the senator freely admitted. He declared that in order to spare Colonel Burr from using his "favor" challenge, he would himself voluntarily withdraw from the jury panel. For this Burr thanked him, expressing the hope that nobody would think that there was anything personal in all of this. Each of these men was a paragon of politeness.

Colonel Nicholas was not so complacent. Yes, he disliked and distrusted Burr, he said bluntly. For this reason he had suffered some qualms about serving on the grand jury panel, but at last he had decided to do so; but now he would, like Senator Giles, voluntarily withdraw.

The crowd was disappointed.

As foreman, to preside over the fifteen at last selected, the Chief Justice appointed a tall, gawky, flaxen-haired man, a man with weather-tanned face and extraordinarily long legs, a scowler who habitually looked as if he had vinegar in his mouth instead of spit. This was John Randolph of Roanoke, the redoubtable horseman and leader of the "Quids" in the House of Representatives. He was a Democrat, to be sure, but a wildly unpredictable one, and no kowtower to the President, whom he used to refer to as St. Thomas of Cantingbury.

Randolph, like almost all the others, admitted that he had no use for Burr, but he reckoned that he could come up with a fair verdict based on the evidence presented. (Incidentally, he was a second cousin to the Edmund Randolph of Burr's legal staff.)

It was a blue-ribbon jury, an exceptionally fine one. Socially, at least, Aaron Burr could have found no fault with it.

For the most part, that first day, Burr conducted his case with all the confident precision of a Jesuit playing chess; but there was to be one eruption of temper. He had been asking the Chief Justice to instruct the jury in what was and what was not admissible evidence, surely a blameless request. Hay, however, saw fit to break in upon it. The defendant must not ask for special treatment, he insisted. The defendant "stood on the same footing with every other man charged with crime."

"Would to God that I did stand on the same ground with every other man!" Burr cried. "This is the first time that I have been permitted to enjoy the rights of a citizen. How have I been brought hither?" [32]

The Chief Justice, startled, his rhadamanthine calm momentarily broken, rebuked him for this. It was no time to bring up such a matter, the Chief Justice said.

Burr apologized.

It was the defense strategy to impress upon the public—for both sides were talking to the public rather than to the Chief Justice—that Burr had been deprived of his rights, that the United States government—more specifically the Democratic party and the President who controlled it—had deliberately set out to get him convicted, no matter what the evidence. Jefferson was enormously popular, riding the crest of a wave at just this time, and they had to be careful how they jabbed him, as for example, when two days after that opening day outburst, Burr fairly purred:

"The President is a great lawyer. Surely he ought to know what constitutes war? Six months ago he proclaimed that there was a civil war. And yet, for six months they have been hunting for it and cannot find one spot where it existed. There was, to be sure, a most terrible war in the newspapers; but nowhere else."

He was not called upon to apologize for that one.

Now they had their fine grand jury, but they could not do any indicting. The government did not have a star witness.

At first the government case had rested largely on the depositions of Wilkinson and Eaton, but Eaton's was entirely hearsay, and since that time the man had made such a spectacle of himself in the streets and barrooms of Richmond, with his sash and his ridiculous hat (and he was drunk most of the time, too) that his evidence could be discounted in advance. That left Wilkinson; and where *was* Wilkinson? Presumably he was coming by sea, but no one could be sure of it.

Hay, in all seriousness, pointed out that allowances should be made for a man of the General's "age and bulk," bringing hoots of derision from the defense.

Meanwhile, the grand jury was recessed time after time, for a day each time at first, but soon it was recessed for a whole week.

To fill the interval, and to look busy, Hay came up with a proposal that rocked the defense. He said he thought that the Chief Justice should at this stage of the trial commit the defendant on a charge of treason, as he had refused to do after the arraignment, instead of on just a charge of high misdemeanor, as the case now stood. His reason for this, he said, was that between the arraignment and the start of the trial proper—a matter of some seven weeks—the diligent government had collected from beyond the mountains a great deal of additional evidence, which it was now prepared to submit.

The defense objected. Ben Botts accused the prosecution of deceit, for he said that each side had agreed in advance not to spring any surprises without consulting the other side. Randolph announced that in thirty years of law practice in Virginia he had never heard of such a thing. Lee and Wickham suggested an off-the-record conference; and this was held, but it resulted in nothing.

John Marshall, frankly, was uncertain of himself here.

He asked the lawyers to argue. They obliged—at length. He listened to every word, never showing a sign of impatience or weariness.

There was a District Court judge sitting beside the Chief Justice, Cyrus Griffin, but he had nothing to do either. He was there only in his *amicus curiae* capacity, and John Marshall consulted him only once in the course of the entire trial, and then only briefly on a minor legal technicality.

"You can little conceive the talents for procrastination that have been exhibited in this affair," a young man named Washington Irving, who was down from New York to cover the trial for a paper there, wrote to a friend. "Day after day we have been disappointed by the nonarrival of the magnanimous Wilkinson; day after day have fresh murmurs and complaints been uttered; and day after day are we told that the next mail will probably bring this noble self, or at least some account of when he may be expected." [33]

The Chief Justice, after hearing everything, took a night to think it over, and returned to court the next morning with a long written decision, which he read. He had decided against the defense, and for the government. He had decided, he said in many words, that he did after all have authority to commit the prisoner on another charge even though the trial had started—provided, always, that the forthcoming evidence justified such a commitment.

Hay said, candidly, that his chief purpose in making this move had been to get the defendant's bail raised. The defense had hinted that perhaps General Wilkinson would never appear at all, that rather than face Aaron Burr in open court, and knowing that many men believed *him* guilty of conspiracy and treason, he might bolt to another country. George Hay now threw this back at the defense. What if *Burr*, afraid to face *Wilkinson*, should bolt to another country?

Colonel Burr did not even honor this suggestion with a sniff, but his attorneys fought on, never giving an inch, and at last, after much more verbal backing and filling, Justice Marshall doubled the bail, making it a total of $20,000.

Once again, and in spite of his earlier fears, Burr had no trouble raising the money. His counsel at the previous hearing had asserted that he had few friends in Richmond, fewer than anywhere else in the country; and that might have been true—then. It was true no longer. Making friends was what Aaron Burr did best. Perhaps a mite timorously at first, but with increasing enthusiasm, Richmond folks had taken him up. He was a lion.

A last-minute contribution of $2,000 cash, right out of the pocket of still another lawyer, came when Luther Martin arrived, May 28, from Baltimore.

Martin was thought by many to be the best barrister in the land. A sexagenarian, he was full of fire, irascible, learned, dogged, sloppy, rough. It was said of him that if he ever got sober he would collapse; but there seemed little likelihood of such an occurrence in the foreseeable future. He always carried a supply with him, even into the courtroom, and was known in the profession as Old Brandy Bottle. Yet he never slurred his words, never lurched or reeled, and never missed a legal trick.

He had come to serve in Aaron Burr's counsel for two reasons: he hated Thomas Jefferson and he was in love—at his age!—with Theodosia.

Jefferson had called this man "an unprincipled and impudent federal bull-dog," [34] and was to suggest, soon, in a letter to Hay, that Martin be indicted with Burr as *particeps criminis*; but it was generally conceded that, though he might be vulgar, he was an authentic genius, and any fight he was in would be a good fight.

17

Despite the long decisions that Justice Marshall would read in a low, flat, emotionless voice—they sometimes went on for three hours—and despite too the technicalities about which the lawyers argued (it would seem interminably), the Hall of Delegates was filled every day.

The audience stayed about the same, consisting mostly of small farmers and backwoodsmen in homespun and buckskin, who were for Jefferson to a man, and a smattering of poised, elegant, snuff-taking swells, who for the most part, though quiet about it, approved of Colonel Burr, who after all *was* a gentleman.

Burr had a much more outspoken advocate in the person of long lank Andrew Jackson, his host more than once at The Hermitage. Because of those visits the government had decided to summon Jackson as a witness, but it was soon to learn its mistake. Jackson, unheard of in Richmond, was strong for Aaron Burr, and he didn't mind saying so, haranguing any street crowd that could be collected. He couldn't abide that man Wilkinson. Neither did he have any respect for President Jefferson, who was proposing, the fool, to spend $2,-

000,000 to buy the Floridas. Andrew Jackson would just have *taken* them.

The government soon decided to let General Jackson go back to Nashville, Tennessee, without having taken the witness stand.[35]

It was now up to the defense to toss a lighted grenade into the circus ring, and Colonel Burr elected to do this in person. Tuesday, June 9, he rose to propose that President Jefferson be served with a *duces tecum* subpoena requiring him to come into court with certain papers Burr said were important to his case, including the original of the letter Wilkinson had written to the President October 21, 1806, the letter the President had quoted in his special message to Congress. Burr also demanded copies of the orders with reference to himself which had been issued by the navy and the army, copies he said he had asked for in vain.

This caused a great stir in the ranks of the prosecution, and a very volcano of protests. Could the President of the United States be summoned into court just like any ordinary citizen? Would he consent to accept such a subpoena? *Should* he?

On the other hand, if he refused to obey the subpoena would it not look as though he was deliberately persecuting Aaron Burr, something that folks were beginning to suspect anyway?

Great men make great mistakes; and Thomas Jefferson here was suffering from the effects of one of his greatest, a whopper.

The discussion lasted several days. Did the Court have the *authority* to issue such an order to the President of the United States? Justice Marshall heard arguments on both sides, slept on it, and the next day read his written opinion. He had decided that he did have that authority.

Hay attempted to pooh-pooh the whole thing, calling it a waste of time, a remark that brought snorts of indignation from defense counsel. Just who was *he*, Wickham asked him to his face, to speak of wasting time? Wickham accused him of using delaying tactics while he waited for orders from the White House; and that this charge was true only made it sting the more.

The lawyers were beginning to snarl at one another now, which was the way it should be. The crowd loved it.

It was Old Brandy Bottle who starred in this debate. He talked all one afternoon, and the spectators wouldn't have missed a word of it.

Just who was this President? demanded Martin. Was he "some kind of sovereign?" No. He was no more than a servant of the people, and when the people speak should he not obey?

"This is a peculiar case," the man from Baltimore thundered. "The President has undertaken to prejudice my client by declaring that 'of his guilt there can be no doubt.' He has assumed to himself the knowledge of the Supreme Being, and pretended to search the heart of my highly respected friend. He has pronounced him a traitor in the face of that country, which has rewarded him. He has let slip the dogs of war, the hellhounds of persecution, to hunt down my friend. . . . And would this President of the United States, who has raised all this absurd clamor, pretend to keep back the papers which are wanted for this trial, where life itself is at stake . . . Whoever withholds willfully information that would save the life of a person charged with a capital offense, is substantially a murderer, and so recorded in the register of Heaven." [36]

Burr had signed an affidavit attesting that the papers in question were material to his case, but in fact they weren't any such thing, and the whole business was simply a trick to embarrass the President. John Marshall did issue the *duces tecum* order, but he caused to have written into it assurance that the papers in question "will be admitted [to court] as sufficient observance of the process, without the personal attendance of any or either of the persons therein named." Thus, Thomas Jefferson never did defy the Supreme Court, as some historians had credited him with doing.

The subpoena had just been sent, and the trial looked to be about to return to that tedious round of speeches concerning the nature and legal definition of treason by means of which the lawyers on both sides were wont to mark time, when the arrival of General Wilkinson himself perked things up.

It was Saturday, June 13, and he came by coach from Norfolk, where his ship had anchored the previous night. He was followed by a crowd of aides and secretaries and witnesses, and they all put up at the Golden Eagle (Burr had left that hotel some time before, and was now staying with friends).

Wilkinson did not appear on Sunday, and it was given out that he was "fatigued"; but Monday morning, in all the glory of gold braid and sword, plumed hat and oversized epaulettes, he presented himself in the Hall of Delegates.

There are two versions of this famous confrontation. One is Wilkinson's own, in a letter to the President:

He said he "darted a flash of indignation at the little Traitor—This Lyon hearted Eagle Eyed Hero, sinking under the weight of conscious guilt, with haggard Eye, made an Effort to meet the indignant salutation of outraged Honor, but it was in vain, his audacity failed Him, He averted his face, grew pale & affected passion to conceal his perturbation." [37]

Washington Irving, who had "secured a good place" in

anticipation of this very meeting, saw it differently:

"Burr was seated with his back to the entrance, facing the judge, and conversing with one of his counsel. Wilkinson strutted into the Court, and took a stand in a parallel line with Burr on his right hand. Here he stood for a moment swelling like a turkey cock, and bracing himself up for the encounter of Burr's eye. The latter did not take any notice of him until the judge directed the clerk to swear General Wilkinson; at the mention of the name Burr turned his head, looked him full in the face with one of his piercing regards, swept his eye over his whole person from head to foot, as if to scan its dimensions, and then coolly resumed his former position, and went on conversing with his counsel as tranquilly as ever. The whole look was over in an instant; but it was an admirable one." [38]

18

THE DAYS WERE mercilessly hot, but the crowd never fell off. Men would wait hours to get into the Hall of Delegates.

The grand jury gave General Wilkinson a hard time. These jurors were busy men, important men, planters or politicians or both, and they did not enjoy waiting for weeks on end while an overfed soldier fumbled his way around Florida. It is true that they had been dismissed for one whole week, to give them a chance, as Washington Irving put it, to "go home, see their wives, get their clothes washed, and flog their negroes," but nevertheless a vast amount of their time had been wasted.

There was more to it than that. The General might have been mildly impressive at a distance, what with his thunderous orders and the vaporings of his letters, but seen close up he was, for all his fat, transparent. He was a miserable self-seeker, as these men of higher-than-average intelligence at once saw.

More, the General, like any good liar, had first convinced

himself that what he said was true. He *did* believe that he, single-handedly and at a great personal risk, had saved the nation. He still liked to be called the "Washington of the West." Some shortcomings James Wilkinson might have had, but self-depreciation was not one of them.

Randolph of Roanoke, the acidulous foreman, punctured his pomposity the moment he came into the grand jury room. Randolph looked at him, looked at his sword, and summoned a bailiff.

"Take that man out and disarm him. I will allow no attempt to intimidate the jury."

They kept him there for four days, and these must have been highly uncomfortable days for the General, who was made to sweat in more ways than one. He was to complain, almost tearfully, in a letter to Thomas Jefferson; and the President was to reply deploring "the injustice which has been aimed at you," and begging the General to accept his "salutations and assurances of respect and esteem."

Grand jury proceedings are traditionally secret, but there were all sorts of leaks in this case, and whatever went on inside was known outside only a few minutes later.

The General showed the jury what he said was the self-same letter that Samuel Swartwout had delivered to him in the camp at Natchitoches, but he was obliged to confess that he had tampered with it, scratching out a word here and there and substituting other words, erasing the entire first sentence. There were jurors who believed that he had written the whole thing in the first place, and that he was at least as guilty as Burr, possibly more so. To these it seemed patent that he was telling the story he told, hanging his former partner, purely and simply in order to save his own fat neck. These jurors would have indicted the General as well as Aaron Burr.

Others dissented. They might not believe General Wilkinson, but it was an elementary rule of drama not to have *two* villains. If Wilkinson was indicted for misprision of treason, as these men proposed, it would have shifted some of the public abhorrence to him from Burr, which would make it that much harder to convict Burr, not to mention what it would do to the confidence of the populace in its army.

When it came to a vote, there were seven grand jurors in favor of indicting Wilkinson, nine opposed. It had been a near thing.

The jury heard other witnesses, about fifty in all, but did not spend much time on them, for they were a sorry lot.

There were some who, like Andrew Jackson, were emphatically pro-Burr.

There were some who, like the two servants from Blennerhassett Island, could only repeat grandiose but vague scraps of overheard talk about making Burr the Emperor of Mexico.

There were some who, like Eaton, had discredited themselves in advance.

There was the national Surveyor of Public Buildings, Benjamin H. Latrobe, who had just finished a model penitentiary for the state of Virginia, near Richmond, but who was in the Capital now because he was known to have had several conferences with Aaron Burr before Burr went west. He testified that those conferences had to do with the feasibility of building a canal around the Ohio River Rapids, a project in which Burr for a long time had been known to be interested.

There was Sergeant Jacob Dunbaugh, who testified that he saw many cases of muskets being heaved into the river after having been made fast to the various boats by means of ropes passed through holes drilled in the sides for that very purpose, just before the searching of Burr's flotilla at Thompson's Bayou—something that nobody else seems to have noticed. The grand jury discounted this, not only because of its fantastic improbability but also because Dunbaugh was facing Army charges of desertion.

In short, it was Wilkinson's testimony, almost alone, that caused the grand jury to bring in indictments; but bring them in they did, June 24, finding, as the clerk read it:

"An indictment against Aaron Burr for treason.
An indictment against Aaron Burr for misdemeanor.
An indictment against Harman Blennerhassett for treason.
An indictment against Harman Blennerhassett for misdemeanor."

Burr listened without any expression. He would have thought it vulgar to show emotion, no matter what he might have felt. Blennerhassett too remained, for him, almost impassive. Cleared in Mississippi, Blennerhassett had been arrested when he returned to his island in the Ohio, and he was now in court, a co-defendant with Burr. These two were no longer cordial. Blennerhassett was sore about a matter of $21,000 which he said he had lent to Burr, a loan that was underwritten by Burr's son-in-law Joseph Alston, who seemed reluctant to make it good.

Randolph of Roanoke still was not satisfied.

"The mammoth of iniquity escaped," he wrote to a friend.[39] "Wilkinson is the only man I ever saw who was from the bark to the very core a villain. . . . Perhaps you never saw human nature in so degraded a situation as in the person of Wilkinson before the grand jury, and yet this man stands on the very summit and pinnacle of executive favor."

The next day the same grand jury returned similar indictments against Jonathan Dayton, John Smith, Comfort Tyler, Israel Smith, and Davis Floyd, all men prominent in business or politics or both, and all associated with Aaron Burr.

The grand jury was dismissed, and Justice Marshall set August 3 as the day for the trial to start and ordered the United States Marshal to prepare a panel of 48 men to report that day, from which panel, it was hoped, the 12 petit jurors would be picked.

Treason is not a bailable offense, and now that Aaron Burr was under indictment, it would not be legal to allow him his freedom. The Chief Justice, that same afternoon of the day the grand jury reported, accordingly sentenced him to an indeterminate term in Richmond jail, which, even as city jails went, was notably filthy. He was put into a small cell with a man and a woman. He did not complain.

His lawyers *did* complain, contending that the city establishment was bad for his health and that there were no accommodations there to allow him to confer with his counsel. Justice Marshall gave permission for the prisoner to live in chambers on the second floor of a house Luther Martin had rented across Broad Street from the Swan Hotel, provided that the door was padlocked and the windows double-shuttered, while the premises were patrolled night and day by seven guards.

This arrangement did not last long. Hay, though he had agreed to it in the first place, and though the Surveyor of Public Buildings himself had inspected the Martin place and avouched it to be practically breakproof, now made complaint that it was showing favor to the prisoner.

Governor Cabell came to the rescue of a distressed federal government by offering it the temporary use of the brand-new state penitentiary, an offer the federal government gratefully accepted.

Burr's new quarters were again on the second floor, but this was a grander building and out in the country. He seems not to have suffered any inconvenience. Not only his lawyers

THEODOSIA ALSTON.

but the ladies of the town visited him in droves, bringing jams, soups, fruits, sweetmeats. A large body of young men went to court with him each morning and back each night, as a sort of honor guard.

Theodosia Alston would have come to her father's side as soon as she learned that he had been arrested, but he forbade this, so she remained on the banks of the Waccamaw far away. Now, however, he thought that it might be pleasant to have her here and to introduce her into Richmond society, so he wrote her to come. She came right away, bringing her husband, and *they* took the quarters in Luther Martin's house that had been thought too luxurious for Burr, though in truth Theo spent most of her time at the penitentiary acting as her father's hostess and secretary. She was a great hit with the local elite, as he of course had known she would be.

19

THE WEATHER went on being torrid. Nobody could remember such a hot summer. Tempers were frayed. Young Swartwout, encountering General Wilkinson in the town, shoved him off the sidewalk. Wilkinson refused to challenge, so *Swartwout* challenged *him*. The General haughtily replied that he would have no correspondence with traitors, after which Swartwout posted him as "a coward & a Poltroon." [40]

Wilkinson himself tried to challenge John Wickham for having called him a perjurer in open court, but Wickham refused to accept the challenge on the ground that an offense that can be taken to law is not an offense suitable to take to the field of honor. Wilkinson did not sue.

It required two whole weeks to pick a petit jury. Only four were taken from the first venire, none at all from the second, and eight from the third, since by that time everybody was tired of the process. Burr himself admitted that it would be impossible to find twelve men who had no prejudice in this much-publicized case. The only peremptory challenge he used was for a venireman named Hamilton. The Chief Justice allowed this.

The jury was sworn August 17. The foreman was Colonel Edward Carrington, a brother-in-law of Chief Justice Marshall.

Section 3 of Article 3 of the United States Constitution reads: "Treason against the United States shall consist only in levying war against them, or in adhering to their enemies, giving them aid and comfort. No person shall be convicted of treason unless on the testimony of two witnesses to the same overt act, or on confession in open court. The Congress shall have power to declare the punishment of treason, but no attainder of treason shall work corruption of blood or forfeiture except during the life of the person attainted."

Since the United States had no enemy at the time of the Burr conspiracy, the "aid and comfort" phrase meant nothing, and Burr, if he was to be found guilty of treason, must be found guilty of levying war against the United States, a difficult thing to prove.

The defense contended that no overt act had been committed, or at least that none could be proved.

This started the so-called Great Debate, August 20, the seventeenth day of the trial. It was to continue for nine days.

Meanwhile witnesses were being heard, but they were the same witnesses the grand jury had questioned, and their stories were familiar.

Part of the prosecution's strategy was to split the defense, and with this in mind President Jefferson took the extraordinary step of sending a batch of blank pardons to George Hay to distribute as he thought best. Hay did offer one to Dr. Bollman, who indignantly refused it.

A more sensational move came when the dashing William Wirt gave forth with a florid address concentrated largely upon Harman Blennerhassett. The ostensible purpose of this address was to spike the report that Blennerhassett was the real leader, Burr only a lieutenant. Its actual purpose un-doubtedly was to paint Burr even blacker than he had pre-viously been painted, and perhaps to get Blennerhassett feel-ing so sorry for himself that he might testify against his partner. On this last point it failed; but it went on for hours, and the listeners thought it the high point of the trial.

"Let us put the case between Burr and Blennerhassett. Let us compare the two men and settle this question of precedence between them. It may save a good deal of trouble-some ceremony hereafter.

"Who Aaron Burr is, we have seen in part already. I will add, that beginning his operations in New York, he associates with him men whose wealth is to supply the necessary funds. Possessed of the main spring, his personal labor contrives all the machinery. Pervading the continent from New York to New Orleans, he draws into his plan, by every allurement which he can contrive, men of all ranks and descriptions. To youthful order he presents danger and glory; to ambition, rank, and titles, and honors; to avarice, the mines of Mexico. To each person whom he addresses he presents the object adapted to his taste. His recruiting officers are appointed. Men are engaged throughout the continent. Civil life is indeed quiet upon its surface, but in its bosom this man has contrived to deposit the materials which, with the slightest touch of his match, produce an explosion to shake the continent. All this his restless ambition has contrived; and in the autumn of 1806 he goes forth for the last time to apply this match. On this occasion he meets with Blennerhassett."

He paused; he drew a deep breath; and then he really outdid himself.

"Who is Blennerhassett? A native of Ireland, a man of letters, who fled from the storms of his own country to find quiet in ours. His history shows that war is not the natural element of his mind. If it had been, he never would have exchanged Ireland for America. So far is an army from furnishing the society natural and proper to Mr. Blennerhassett's character, that on his arrival in America, he retired even from the population of the Atlantic States, and sought quiet and solitude in the bosom of our western forests. But he carried with him taste, and science, and wealth; and lo, the desert smiled! Possessing himself of a beautiful island in the Ohio, he rears upon it a palace and decorates it with every romantic embellishment of fancy. A shrubbery that Shenstone might have envied blooms around him. Music that might have charmed Calypso and her nymphs is his. An extensive library spreads its treasures before him. A philosophical apparatus offers him all the secrets and mysteries of nature. Peace, tranquillity, and innocence shed their mingled delights around him. And to crown the enchantment of the scene, a wife, who is said to be lovely even beyond her sex, and graced with every accomplishment that can render it irresistible, had blessed him with her love and made him the father of several children. The evidence would convince you that this is but a faint picture of the real life. In the midst of all this peace, this innocent simplicity and this tranquillity, this feast of the mind, this pure banquet of the heart, the destroyer comes; he comes to change this paradise into a hell. Yet the flowers do not wither at his approach. No monitory shuddering through the bosom of their unfortunate possessor warns him of the ruin that is coming upon him. A stranger presents himself. Introduced to their civilities by the high rank which he had lately held in his country, he soon finds his way to their hearts, by the dignity and elegance of his demeanor, the light and beauty of his conversation, and the seductive and fascinating power of his address. The conquest was not difficult. Innocence is ever simple and credulous. Conscious of no design itself, it suspects none in others. It wears no guard before his breast. Every door and portal and avenue of the heart is thrown open, and all who choose it enter. Such was the state of Eden when the serpent entered its bowers. The prisoner, in a more engaging form, winding himself into the open and unpracticed heart of the unfortunate Blennerhassett, found but little difficulty in changing the native character of that heart and the objects of its affection. By degrees he infuses into it the poison of his own ambition. He breathes into it the fire of his own courage; a daring and desperate thirst for glory; an ardor panting for great enterprises, for all the storm, and bustle, and hurricane of life. In a short time the whole man is changed, and every object of his former delight is relinquished. No longer he enjoys the tranquil scene: it has become flat and insipid to his taste. His books are abandoned. His retort and crucible are thrown aside. His shrubbery blooms and breathes its fragrance upon the air in vain: he likes it not. His ear no longer drinks the rich melody of music; it longs for the trumpet's clangor and the cannon's roar. Even the prattle of his babes, once so sweet, no longer affects him; and the angel smile of his wife, which hitherto touched his bosom with ecstacy so unspeakable, is now unseen and unfelt. Greater objects have taken possession of his soul. His imagination has been dazzled by visions of diadems, of stars and garters, and titles of nobility. He has been taught to burn with restless emulation at the names of great heroes and conquerors. His enchanted island is destined soon to relapse into a wilderness; and in a few months we find the beautiful and tender partner of his bosom whom he lately 'permitted not the winds of' summer 'to visit too roughly,' we find her shivering at midnight, on the winter banks of the Ohio, and mingling her tears with the torrents, those froze as they fell. Yet this unfortunate man, thus deluded from his interest and his happiness, thus seduced from the paths of innocence and peace, thus confounded in the toils that were deliberately spread for him and overwhelmed by the mastering spirit and genius of another—this man, thus ruined and undone, and made to play a subordinate part in this grand drama of guilt and treason— this man is to be called the principal offender, while *he*, by whom he was thus plunged into misery, is comparatively innocent, a mere accessory! Is this reason? Is it law? Is it humanity? Sir, neither the human heart nor the human understanding will bear a perversion so monstrous and absurd! so shocking to the soul! so revolting to reason!"

There was more, much more.

The speech was accepted as an American classic, and it soon found its way into the schoolbooks, so that many a lad was obliged to memorize it, in whole or at least the part quoted above, and to recite this on important occasions. It became what, a little later, Daniel Webster's Bunker Hill monument speech became, and, later still, the much more worthy Lincoln's Gettysburg Address. It did nothing to elucidate any point of law, and nothing, surely, to sway the mind of the Chief Justice or the minds of the jurymen, but it did enchant a whole generation of Americans, and though Aaron Burr himself would laugh at it,[41] the speech undoubtedly did more to besmirch his name than anything else in his life, even including the duel with Alexander Hamilton.

20

SUCH SHENANIGANS as those of William Wirt—and, a little later, on the other side, those of Benjamin Botts—were not characteristic of the proceedings. There were farcical elements in the Burr trial, but the trial *as* a trial was no farce. It was a serious, determined, and learned attempt to define treason in the United States for the benefit of future generations, and either to undermine or to bolster the power of the Supreme Court. The nation was young, scarcely thirty years of age, and whatever conclusions these men arrived at, whatever precedents they set, would be of incalculable importance to posterity. They knew this.

What the government had to do was prove that Burr, Blennerhassett, and sundry others had raised an army, or prepared to do so, had used force, or threatened to use force, specifically on the night of December 10, 1806, at Blennerhassett Island. It was easily proved that Burr himself was not on the island that night—he was, in fact, at Frankfort, Kentucky—but it was contended that his physical presence was not needed to make up an act of treason. English precedents were cited by both sides on this point.

Even the indictment described the crowd on Blenner-hassett Island that night—the largest ever assembled there—as "thirty persons or upwards," and there was a split of opinion as to whether it could be called martial. A couple of snoopers from the mainland testified that they *thought* they saw muskets, though it was so dark that they could not be sure of this, and that they heard cries they *thought* were the challenges of sentries; but another man actually visited the island that night, and he testified that he was never accosted and that he saw only a few guns such as might be carried by any group of men about to drop down the river.

Burr interrupted this with the assertion that it was inadmissible, being collateral, not direct. In other words, such testimony could not in itself establish that an overt act had been committed, and without the establishment of an overt act there was no case.

Justice Marshall heard him out, but permitted a few more witnesses, being, as he always was in this trial, unwilling to give any appearance of one-sidedness,[42] until at last, August 20, Wickham put this contention in the form of a motion, which meant that the Chief Justice would be obliged to give a decision.

Upon this decision everything would hang; for if John Marshall decreed that only he, and not the jury, should pronounce testimony admissible or inadmissible, and if he ruled out the sort of evidence that had already been given—and the government had more of the same but nothing stronger—then the prosecution was finished.

This was the Great Debate; and though it did have a few light moments, it was for the most part a grim, even bitter, if inconscionably long-winded affair. Most of the speeches were addressed not to the audience or even to the jury but directly and emphatically to John Marshall himself.

The debate lasted until the close of court Saturday, August 29, at which time Justice Marshall announced that he would read his decision first thing Monday morning. He would be uncommonly careful about this, as everybody knew. He could feel Thomas Jefferson's breath on the back of his neck.

He took his time, and read every word of it, the longest decision in the history of American jurisprudence, and one which was to stand as the official definition of treason for 110 years.[43]

Painstakingly he went over all the arguments that all the clever lawyers had made. He quoted copiously, citing many authorities.

It was nine o'clock when he started. It was a little after noon when he finished with:

"The result of the whole is a conviction as complete as the mind of the Court is capable of receiving on a complex subject, that the motion must prevail."

In other words, unless the government could produce some new testimony of another type, the case would go to the jury as it stood.

George Hay, though he must have known that he was licked, asked for time to think it over. This was granted. Any extra time that any lawyer in that trial asked for was always granted.

Next morning Hay admitted that he could think of nothing further. The case went to the jury, which was out only twenty-five minutes. A clerk read the verdict the foreman had handed to him:

"We of the jury say that Aaron Burr is not proved to be guilty under this indictment by any evidence submitted to us. We, therefore, find him not guilty."

Instantly the defense was on its feet. What kind of a Scotch verdict was this? It was altogether improper. The jury's duty, and its *only* duty, was to find a verdict of guilty or else a verdict of not guilty. Anything else was irregular and indeed illegal.

The Justice, after some further wrangling, ordered the verdict to be entered in the record as simply "not guilty."

The rest is anticlimax.

A spell of thunderstorms had broken the heat wave, but when the storms were past the heat came back worse than ever, and with it came an influenza epidemic. Harman Blennerhassett was prostrated, but none of the other principals was touched.

For the case dragged on, though the issue was no longer in doubt. There was still the indictment for high misdemeanor to be dealt with, and whether or not George Hay might think longingly of an end to the strife he had his orders—straight from the White House. It would be impossible, now, to convict Aaron Burr, but it might still be possible to catch John Marshall in a misstep.

Aaron Burr was bailed again, after having spent almost nine weeks in what he called the Emperor's Palace, and he went to live with his daughter and son-in-law opposite the Swan; and Harman Blennerhassett was absent, being sick; but otherwise everything was the same, and the whole tiresome business had to be gone over again, until at last, September 15, a second jury brought in a verdict of simple "not guilty," and that was, indisputably, the end.

21

THE PUBLIC HAD found him guilty, and a little thing like a United States Supreme Court decision was not about to change this. A howl of rage rose when the result was announced, for it was universally supposed that there had been dirty work. (John Marshall, however, was not impeached; there was nothing for which to impeach him.)

Aaron Burr was not safe anywhere in an angry America. For some time he did not dare to show himself in the streets. He could not hope to practice his profession, public feeling being what it was, and the Mexican project was dead—at least, at home. There was an attempt to indict him, and all the others, in Ohio; but this came to nothing.

Burr was an unquenchable optimist; rose-colored glasses were inflexibly fixed upon his nose. He still believed that he could take over Mexico and reign there, if only he had the proper financial backing. The trial was an interruption, but not more. England was the place for him, so he went to England. He sneaked out of New York, slipping aboard a packet in the Lower Bay from a pilot boat chartered for the occasion. He was using the name of H. E. Edwards, as he was often to use aliases in this period of his life; but as soon as he arrived in the British Isles he cast this off and went about as himself.

At once he was launched upon a sea of picnics, unpaid tailors' bills, barmaids and incandescent peeresses, bombazine, pet dogs (he was crazy about animals), oversleeping, bottles of champagne, earls by the score, dukes by the dozen, opera tickets, quizzing glasses, snuff boxes, beavers, and lovely linen neckcloths. Invitations engulfed him, and he was all but smothered by highly placed friends eager to help. He was, definitely, a lion.

He loved this; but it brought no money.

The very day that Burr's ship docked, Joseph Bonaparte rode into Madrid as the King of Spain, which meant that sooner or later, and probably sooner, Great Britain would have to fight France again, for it was incumbent upon Britain to take the part of the ousted Bourbon. In the circumstances, neither side wanted to offend Spain.

Burr traveled around England and Scotland a great deal —he was enthusiastic about Edinburgh—but he did not get a foot closer to Mexico. People were sympathetic, but they did not commit themselves.

He met William Godwin and Charles Lamb and William Cobbett and Jeremy Bentham, with the last of whom he formed a close friendship, living in his house for many months; but Whitehall continued to be cold. Soon, indeed, Whitehall was hinting that Colonel Burr should get out. He attributed this attitude to the pressure of the Jefferson administration back in Washington, and he could have been right. The trouble was, while he wished to go to France, France did not seem eager to welcome him.

He was threatened with deportation—to where?—but he tied up these proceedings for some months by contending that he was entitled to all the rights of a British subject since he had been "born within the King's allegiance" of parents who were British subjects.

At last he was allowed to go, or perhaps forced to go, to Sweden. He wandered through that country and Denmark and Germany for the better part of half a year, a highly unhappy man, short of money, lacking friends, and unfamiliar with the languages.

In time he was admitted to France, to Paris; but he never did manage to get an audience with the Emperor, and Talleyrand pointedly snubbed him.

All of this time he was writing throat-catching letters to Theodosia. There was one time, in England, when he thought that she was about to cross the sea and join him, a possibility that made him ecstatic; but her health fell off, and she stayed in America. Theodosia's husband was by this time the Governor of South Carolina. Burr never was overly fond of that fellow, and now he blamed him, unjustly, for Theodosia's illness.

Burr had collected many antique coins and art objects in the course of his travels, meaning to give these to Theodosia and to her son, his beloved grandchild, Aaron Burr Alston, known in the family as "Gampy," but gradually he had to sell them in order to keep from starving. There had been times in Germany and Scandinavia, and there were to be many more times in Paris, when he came close indeed to death, living on a potato and water, while he shivered for lack of firewood. He never complained. Probably he never even *thought* of complaining.

He sought out, in Paris, a protégé from New York, young John Vanderlyn, who was doing well as a portrait painter. Burr had helped him to get his start; but now he was obliged to borrow money from him.

There were times, too, both in London and in Paris, when he had to hide in his miserable lodgings for fear of bill collectors, and did not dare to venture out of doors until after dark. For one of his sunny nature this was Hades.

When at last he decided that it would be best to go back to America and face whatever was waiting for him, he found that he could not get an American passport. The United States consul in Paris was none other than that sour, vindictive Scot, Alexander MacRae, ex-Lieutenant Governor of Virginia, ex-assistant to the United States Attorney General in Richmond, and *he*, understandably, was not minded to go out of his way to help Aaron Burr.

The thing was managed at last, though only after many delays. He never lost heart. Moreover, he kept up his interest in all sorts of shaky enterprises. He still meant to become emperor of Mexico, but he watched with interest the development of a process that might make vinegar out of tree sap, toyed with the idea of inventing a more efficient steamboat than the one Robert Fulton had recently come up with, looked into Dutch land deals, and, in short, kept busy.

He reached Boston May 4, 1812. There was talk about the possibility of war between Great Britain and the United States, but Burr didn't believe it. A man like James Madison, he said, would never fight.

He now had the name of Adolphus Arnot, and he had let his whiskers grow and was wearing a wig. However, needing money, as always, he revealed his true identity to the president of Harvard, Dr. John Thornton Kirkland, who was persuaded to buy for forty dollars some of Burr's books. He took passage on the sloop *Rose* for Fairfield, Connecticut. He was now using the name De Gamelli—*why*, Heaven alone knows.

It was fascinating to visit near Fairfield, a countryside he was familiar with since boyhood. "I strolled three or four hours round some miles in the neighborhood," he wrote in his private journal.[44] "Every object was as familiar to me as those about Richmond Hill, and the review brought up many pleasant and whimsical associations. At several doors I saw the very lips I had kissed and the very eyes which had ogled me in the persons of their grandmothers about six-and-thirty years ago. I did not venture into any of their houses, lest some of the grandmothers might recollect me."

He was landed in New York late at night on June 7, and went immediately to the Swartwout house at 66 Water Street, where he pounded on the door until a woman in another house shouted through a window that the Swartwouts didn't live there any more and that she did not know where they *did* live now. After that he tried every inn he could find. They were all full. He even thought of curling up on somebody's front porch—he had slept in worse places—but refrained because he feared that the watch might pick him up as a vagrant and haul him to the city jail, where he could be recognized. At last he found an unlicensed innkeeper—really the proprietor of a private house—who for 12 cents gave him room on the floor with five other men. He slept well, too.

Next morning he found the Swartwouts, father and son, at their new home, and they kept him under cover for several weeks while arrangements were made for his resurfacing—creditors talked into agreeing to hold off for a little longer, the federal and state authorities sounded out. An advertisement was put into one of the newspapers saying that Colonel Burr had landed in Boston and was expected soon to return to New York, and this did not seem to cause any undue local stir. The fact is that most folks had forgotten about Colonel Burr, but this it was impossible for him to understand.

When at last it seemed safe, they opened a law office for

him at 9 Nassau Street. Almost from the beginning the place
was busy. People *did* remember that, no matter what else
they might think of him, Aaron Burr happened to be one of
the best lawyers in the business. He began to pay off some
of his most pressing debts. He also began to make new ones.

Only a few days after the new office opened, his grandson, Gampy his namesake, died suddenly of fever down in
South Carolina. It was a crushing blow.

Governor Alston could not leave the state—this was
South Carolina law—but it was agreed that Theodosia would
visit her father in New York. They had not seen one another
in more than four years. Theodosia was adjudged not strong
enough to make the trip by land, so she signed as a passenger
aboard the fast privateer, *Patriot*. The ship went down in a
storm off Cape Hatteras.

For weeks after the news came, Aaron Burr, always a
small man and now so tiny that he looked as if he might be
blown away like a straw, paced the sea wall by the Battery
at the lower tip of Manhattan, straining his eyes in the direction of the Narrows, still hoping, somehow, that there would
come news that Theodosia had been rescued and taken to
Bermuda. At last he gave up.

(The wild rumors that she had been captured by pirates
were a later development. Burr himself never heard them.)

He did not give up living. He greeted all sorts of war
companions, often giving them money. In 1822 he took in
Luther Martin, Old Brandy Bottle, the wreck of a man; and
he kept him for the rest of Martin's life. He continued to be
interested in politics, though he no longer took an active part.

His walks were famous. He was pointed out, a sight. He
was a kindly man, if devious, and he could not bear to hear a
child cry. His pockets were always full of candy, which he
passed out as he walked. He was always beautifully dressed,

and a smile never ceased to twitch the corners of his mouth.

The news about the revolt in Texas thrilled him. "There, you see? I was right!" he cried. "I was only thirty years too soon! What was treason thirty years ago is patriotism now!"

He was careful not to speak to an adult until spoken to. There were still those who would have no part of the murderer of Alexander Hamilton, and he hated scenes. Once, forgetting, he encountered Henry Clay in the street. Clay had suffered, or thought that he had suffered, because he defended Aaron Burr in Kentucky. Impulsively now the Colonel extended his hand. Clay looked at the hand—and walked past.[45]

22

WEDNESDAY, July 3, 1833, Aaron Burr married again.
The semilegendary Mme. Jumel was born Eliza Brown
or Bowen in Providence, Rhode Island, and she early made
her way to New York, leaving an illegitimate child behind.
She was very lovely and not at all straight-laced. She had
picked up a little French in the course of a visit to that land
as the mistress of a sea captain, and this conceivably helped
to endear her to that lonesome rich merchant Stephen Jumel,
who was himself of French parentage. Jumel kept her in his
house for four years, even buying her her own carriage, a
gift much resented by the ladies of the town. At the end of
that time she tricked him into marrying her by pretending
that she was at death's door—as, emphatically, she wasn't. He
made the best of his bargain, buying her the Robert Morris
house up in Harlem.

Here was an edifice already distinguished. It had served
as Washington's headquarters while the Continental troops
occupied Manhattan in the Revolution, and later, when the
British were in charge, it was the headquarters of the top-

ranking Hessian officer, Lieutenant General Wilhelm von Knyphausen. Afterward it had rather gone to seed, though it was used as a tavern for a while. Aaron Burr himself, entranced by the site, the view, at one time thought to buy it; but the deal fell through when he learned that he could not get a good price for his Richmond Hill house.

Stephen Jumel bought this place and spent a lot of money on it and gave it to his wife, who now had all the carriages she wanted.[46]

Still she rode alone, she sipped tea alone. The ladies of the town did not come calling. New York was not as moralistically severe as Boston or Philadelphia, but that Brown woman had gone too far. At last, bored—Jumel had retired by this time—they went to Europe, where Eliza had a real whirl and was made much of. Jumel lost most of his money, so that after they returned, he was to live out the last years of his life as her guest, for she still had *her* money. She was a termagant, and treated him, according to popular rumor, like a lackey. He died, a broken man, about a year before Burr married Eliza, the richest widow in town.

Burr was seventy-seven, she was fifty-seven. They might or might not have had an affair in the past, when Eliza was accessible and Colonel Burr a gay widower. It was certainly the fashionable belief that they had. "Wednesday, July 3," Philip Hone, an ex-mayor, wrote in his diary.[47] "The celebrated Col. Burr was married on Monday evening to the equally celebrated Mrs. Jumel, widow of Stephen Jumel. It is benevolent in her to keep the old man in his latter days. One good turn deserves another." There were many who thought that.

Now, indubitably, whatever they had been before, they were married. The ceremony was performed at the Jumel Mansion, by the Reverend Dr. Bogart, the same wine-loving clergyman who had married Aaron Burr to another widow,

Mrs. Theodosia Prevost, fifty years before. It was witnessed only by Nelson and Mary Chase, the bride's nephew and his wife, unless, to be sure, some of the eight house servants were eavesdropping. It was followed by a jolly supper.

In the morning, these two took off for Connecticut in a bright yellow carriage. They visited various places, and were made much of. At Hartford they were received by the governor, a cousin of Aaron Burr, and it was there too that Eliza looked into one of her investments, a toll bridge over the Connecticut River. She was not pleased with what she saw, and with Burr's advice she decided to sell her shares for $6,000—a mistake, as it proved. When they proffered her the check, she waved it away. "Give it to my husband," she said grandly. That was another mistake. Aaron Burr never took long getting rid of money. This particular sum he sank into a scheme for settling German immigrants in the West. He was always interested in western settlement projects. This one, like so many others, came to nothing.

There were many occasions like this, and Eliza did not like them. Careless as she might have been in some respects, and liberal, Eliza was always acutely aware of money. Within four months of the time of their return to Harlem, the little colonel was packing his personal belongings into a hired carriage—not the giddy yellow one—in preparation for a departure from the Jumel Mansion. She had kicked him out.

He took refuge with one of his illegitimate sons, a silversmith in Manhattan.

June 12, 1834, Eliza filed suit for absolute divorce, alleging that Burr had been guilty of infidelity "at divers times with divers females," and specifically mentioning one Jane McManus of Jersey City.

Burr denied the charges only informally. He was a good-natured man, this grandson of Jonathan Edwards. "You

THE LAST DAYS OF AARON BURR.

know," he used to say when warned that it might not go well with him after death, "I think that God is a great deal better than some people suppose."

He was reproached when he recognized as his own a child who must have been conceived while he was bedridden. Any woman who honored him by calling him the father of his child, he replied, *should* be treated with consideration. This particular baby he settled an income upon, and he even remembered it in his will, though he was to leave nothing but debts.

Eliza hired as her lawyer Alexander Hamilton, Jr., and on September 14, 1836, Judge Philo T. Ruggles granted her a divorce.

On that very same day the eighty-one-year-old Aaron Burr, still smiling a little, died in the home of some friends on Staten Island.

He was buried in Princeton near the graves of his father and grandfather.

He was one of history's greatest losers. He had lost his mother and his father before he was two years old. He lost his health in the Revolution. He lost the Presidency by one vote, and later lost the governorship of New York, together with control of the party machinery there. He won the duel with Hamilton, but as a result of this "victory" he lost tremendously in prestige and in his profession. He lost his great gamble in the West. He lost his only daughter, his only grandchild as well. He lost more fortunes than he could conveniently count, for they slipped through his hands like cakes of wet soap.

But Aaron Burr never seemed to mind. He kept smiling. He had a wonderful time.

NOTES

1. The reference in those days was always to "the Floridas." They were under separate governments. East Florida was almost exactly the same, territorially, as the present state. West Florida was a continuation of this in the direction indicated, and consisted of the land between the 32nd parallel of latitude and the Gulf of Mexico, or approximately the bottom third of the present states of Alabama and Mississippi. It was generally assumed by Americans that sooner or later they would come into possession of both, but East Florida was not of immediate importance, while West Florida was. The settlers along the Tombigbee and Alabama rivers did not fancy the thought that a foreign power controlled the mouths of these and similar streams and might at any time cut off those settlers' one real exit to the world of commerce.

2. This was the party founded by Thomas Jefferson, and in 1803 it was generally called the Republican party, though sometimes Republican-Democratic or Democratic-Republican. It became the Democratic party, and for that reason will be so called in this book. It had nothing to do with the current Republican party, the G.O.P., which was not organized until half a century later.

3. "The annexation of Louisiana was an event so portentous as to defy measurement; it gave a new face to politics, and ranked in historical importance next to the Declaration of Independence and the adoption of the Constitution— events of which it was the logical outcome." Henry Adams, *History*, II, 49.

4. From *tertium quid*, for they did indeed constitute a sort of third force, headed by John Randolph. They were Democrats who refused to toe the party line at every division. In New York State, a later generation was to give such independent solons the name of Mugwumps, the prevailing explanation being that a Mugwump was a man who sat on a fence with his mug on one side of it, his wump on the other.

5. The present boundary between the states of Louisiana and Arkansas.

6. Today, respectively, Columbia and Princeton.

7. The man in whose honor Church Street, Manhattan, was named. There was never a church *building* on that street.

8. No sides will be taken here in the dispute that raged for years, and may still be raging in remote corners of libraries, as to whether Hamilton or Burr fired first. We have only the word of the two seconds (Dr. Hosack was still down on the beach, remember), and though they were honorable men they were under tension, so that one, at least, must have become confused. Van Ness attested that Hamilton fired first, and that for an instant he feared that his man had been hit, for he saw Burr sway slightly. Then Burr fired, and Hamilton fell. When Van Ness asked his principal why he had swayed or lurched, Burr replied that there had been a small stone under one of his feet and also that he had not wished to fire until the smoke from Hamilton's pistol had at

least in part cleared away. On the other hand, Judge Pendleton was firm in his assertion that Burr fired first and that Hamilton, hit, must have fired by accident, a muscular reaction. Hamilton had told him that he intended to throw his first shot away, Pendleton said, a course the representative thought ill-advised. Also, Pendleton said, in the boat going back Hamilton through his failing eyes saw the pistol on the planking next to where he lay, and warned against touching it, pointing out that it was loaded, which would seem to argue that he never knew he had fired it. Neither man ever gave an inch in this argument. It scarcely matters, now. There are many excellent accounts of the Burr-Hamilton duel. The reader's attention is called particularly to a compilation of the original documents published in 1960 by the Wesleyan University Press. (See *Bibliography*, under Syrett.)

9. The exact site of the duel has since been blasted away to make room for West Shore Railroad freight yards, but a stone, with a plaque attached stating that it was upon this that Alexander Hamilton rested his head after he fell, has been moved to the top of the cliff, and may still be seen there, surmounted by a small American flag. The author lived near this spot, many years ago, and he could never pass that stone, a large one, without the irreverent reflection that Hamilton must have had a hell of a long neck.

10. The present corner of Varick and Charleton streets.

11. The site today is bounded by Amsterdam Avenue, St. Nicholas Avenue, and 141st and 145th streets.

12. Those same oaks, draped in Spanish moss, are *inside* the city limits now, a part of City Park, far out Esplanade Avenue.

13. The island is still there, but it is much smaller now, the river having washed a great deal of it away.

14. Dayton, Ohio, was to be named after him.

15. This was not named by Pike himself but by a later explorer, Frémont, in his honor.

16. He was to wind up as a night watchman in the Capitol, Washington, D.C.

17. The author writes with conviction. He drove an ambulance over this same route more than once in the course of the Late Unpleasantness.

18. The northern part of the present state of Louisiana.

19. There was no such state as West Virginia then. Despite sundry earlier attempts to establish a "Westsylvania" it was not until Civil War times that the district (which had voted heavily against secession) won its independence—and its name.

20. He was to be killed at Fallen Timbers five years later. A county in Kentucky is named after him.

21. Because of the importance of this letter in the subsequent trial, and indeed in history, it is printed in full as Appendix A. The reader should be warned, however, that there are several versions of it, for Wilkinson was to admit altering it in certain places and he may have made it totally different. We know at least that the whole thing was not a fabrication. Burr himself never denied it, but he never accepted it either. There *was* a letter; but nobody has ever seen either of the originals.

22. It is printed in full as Appendix B.

23. Today Memphis, Tennessee.

24. The reader should perhaps be reminded that in those days, for better or for worse, the militia *was* a militia, strictly a state organization, answerable only to the governor, and not, as it is now, a national guard.

25. Gayarré, *History of Louisiana*, IV, 177.

26. January 28 Wilkinson in New Orleans dispatched

Captain Moses Hook, two lieutenants, and two army surgeons to Washington, Mississippi, with orders to grab Burr somehow and ship him downriver. Nothing was said about dead-or-alive; but perhaps that was not necessary? The men were armed with pistols and knives, but they had no sort of warrant. They were in civilian clothes. They were promised their expenses and, if they succeeded, $5,000. Abernethy, *The Burr Conspiracy*, 218.

27. The southwest corner of the present state of Alabama.

28. He was to become a major general and a big figure in the Mexican War. Both Gainesville, Florida, and Gainesville, Texas, are named after him.

29. "I never believed him [Burr] a fool, but he must be an idiot and a lunitik, if he really planned and attempted to execute such a project as is imputed to him," John Adams wrote to his wife. "But if his guilt is as clear as the noonday sun, the first Magistrate ought not to have pronounced it so before a jury had tried him." *Works*, IX, 15.

30. "The real prosecutor of Aaron Burr, throughout this business, was Thomas Jefferson, President of the United States, who was made President of the United States by Aaron Burr's tact and vigilance, and who was able therefore to wield against Aaron Burr the power and resources of the United States." Parton, *Aaron Burr*, 456–57.

31. Davis, *Memoirs*, II, 405–406.

32. Robertson, *Trial of Aaron Burr*, I, 13. All further quotations from the trial, unless an exception is specifically noted, will be from this source. David Robertson was a Petersburg, Virginia, lawyer (one of his clerks was the enormous young Winfield Scott, who also attended every session of this trial, but who was later to quit the law in favor of the Army) who had developed his own system of shorthand. He took down every word, every day. The result-

ing two volumes do not constitute an *official* record—there is none—but they are just as good. Robertson never took sides.

33. Irving, *Life and Letters*, I, 150–51.

34. *Writings*, V, 98.

35. This hard feeling was mutual, and it was to carry over into the next administration, when Madison, finding himself in the second war with Great Britain, out of loyalty to his former chief withheld Andrew Jackson's military preferment as long as he dared, only appointing him to a big command in time for the clean-up at New Orleans, a battle actually fought after peace had been proclaimed. If Jackson had been made commander in the north, early in the war, the history of the United States and of Canada would most likely be very different.

36. "Never, since the days of Patrick Henry, had Richmond heard such a defiance of power." Beveridge, *John Marshall*, III, 437. But Henry made his memorable "Give me liberty or give me death" speech in St. John's Episcopal Church, a much smaller structure, in March of 1775. The Capitol had not been built then.

37. Beveridge, *Marshall*, III, 457.

38. Irving, *Life and Letters*, I, 153. It is only fair to add, in this connection, that the scrupulously impartial Robertson calls Wilkinson "dignified" and writes of Burr's "haughty mien." It was Washington Irving who did as much as anybody to fasten into the popular mind a picture of James Wilkinson as a buffoon and therefore, presumably, harmless —or at any rate, not capable of any serious harm, scarcely a first-class scoundrel. In his *Knickerbocker's History of New York*, published two years after the trial, it was easy to identify General Jacobus von Poffenberg, who was "booted to the middle, sashed to the chin, collared to the ears, whiskered to the teeth."

39. To Judge Joseph H. Nicholson. Adams, *Randolph*, 219.

40. The practice of "posting" was a Southern one, but Swartwout, though he came from New York, had traveled much in the South, and after all he was *in* Virginia. When a man refused to accept a challenge to a duel the challenger could—if he wished—"post" him by putting advertsements in the newspapers, sticking up stickers on public bulletin boards, passing out handbills, etc., all proclaiming that So-and-So was an ingrate and a craven coward. Honor was thus satisfied.

41. For years afterward Burr would quote it in company, roaring. Parton, *Aaron Burr*, 498–506. Parton makes the point, a sound one, that Burr didn't ruin Blennerhassett at all, for the Irishman would surely have gone through his money very soon anyway, being that kind of man. After the trial he sank everything he had into a cotton plantation, and what really put the finishing touches to his fortune was the embargo Jefferson imposed upon the country in his desperate attempt to stave off a war with Great Britain—a war his successor, James Madison, inherited.

42. "Marshall's conduct of Burr's trial for treason is the one serious blemish in his judicial record." Corwin, *John Marshall and the Constitution*, 111. On the other hand, many respectable commentators, including Marshall's distinguished biographer, Beveridge, think that this was his finest hour.

43. Until the passage of the Espionage Act of June 15, 1917.

44. *Private Journal*, II, 431.

45. Schurz, *Henry Clay*, I, 37.

46. It is still called the Jumel Mansion. It is a museum, located on West 160th Street between St. Nicholas and Edgecombe avenues.

47. *Diary*, I, 98.

APPENDIX A

no date

Letter from Aaron Burr to
General James Wilkinson

"Your letter, postmarked thirteenth May, is received. At length I have obtained funds, and have actually commenced. The Eastern detachments, from different points and under different pretences, will rendezvous on the Ohio first of November. Everything internal and external favors our views. Naval protection of England is secured. Truxtun is going to Jamaica to arrange with the admiral on that station. It will meet us at the Mississippi. England, a navy of the United States, are ready to join, and final orders are given to my friends and followers. It will be a host of choice spirits. Wilkinson shall be second to Burr only; Wilkinson shall dictate the rank and promotion of his officers. Burr will proceed westward first August, never to return. With him goes his daughter; her husband will follow in October, with a corps of worthies. Send forthwith an intelligent and confidential friend with whom Burr may confer; he shall return immediately with further interesting details; this is essential to concert and harmony of movement. Send a list of all persons known to Wilkinson west of the mountains who could be useful, with a note delineating their characters. By your messenger send me four or five commissions of your officers, which you can borrow under any pretence you please; they shall be returned faithfully. Already are orders given to the contractor to forward six months' provisions to points Wilkinson may name; this shall not be used until the last moment, and then under proper injunctions. Our object, my dear friend, is brought to a point so long desired. Burr guarantees the result with his life and honor, with the lives and honor and the fortunes of hundreds, the best blood of our country. Burr's plan of operation is to move down rapidly from the Falls, on the fifteenth of November, with the first five hundred or a thousand men, in light boats now constructing for that purpose; to be at Natchez between the fifth and fifteenth of December, there to meet you; there to determine whether it will be expedient in the first instance to seize on or pass by Baton Rouge. On receipt of this send Burr an answer. Draw on Burr for all expenses, etc. The people of the country to which we are going are prepared to receive us; their agents, now with Burr, say that if we protect their religion, and will not subject them to a foreign Power, that in three weeks all will be settled. The gods invite us to glory and fortune; it remains to be seen whether we deserve the boon. The bearer of this goes express to you. He's a man of inviolable honor and perfect discretion, formed to execute rather than project, capable of relating facts with fidelity, and incapable of relating them otherwise; he is thoroughly informed of the plans and intentions of Burr, and will disclose to you as far as you require, and no further. He has imbibed a reverence for your character, and may be embarrassed in your presence; put him at ease, and he will satisfy you."

APPENDIX B

Proclamation Issued by President Thomas Jefferson
on November 27, 1806.

"Whereas information has been received that sundry persons, citizens of the U.S. or resident within the same, are conspiring & confederating together to begin & set on foot,
provide & prepare the means for a military expedition or
enterprise against the dominions of Spain, against which nation war has not been declared by the constitutional authority
of the U.S.; that for this purpose they are fitting out & arming vessels in the western waters of the U.S., collecting provisions, arms, military stores & other means; are deceiving &
seducing honest & well meaning citizens under various pretences to engage in thier criminal enterprises; are organizing,
officering & arming themselves for the same, contrary to the
laws in such cases made & provided, I have therefore thought
fit to issue this my proclamation, warning and enjoining all
faithful citizens who have been led to participate in the sd
unlawful enterprises without due knolege or consideration to
withdraw from the same without delay & commanding all

persons whatsoever engaged or concerned in the same to cease all further proceedings therein as they will answer the contrary at their peril, and will incur prosecution with all the rigors of the law. And I hereby enjoin and require all officers civil or military, or the U.S. or of any of the states or territories, & especially all governors, & other executive authorities, all judges, justices, and other officers of the peace, all military officers of the army or navy of the U.S., & officers of the militia, to be vigilant, each within his respective department and according to his functions in searching out & bringing to condign punishment all persons engaged or concerned in such enterprise and in seizing & detaining subject to the dispositions, of the law all vessels, arms, military stores, or other means provided or providing for the same, & in general in preventing the carrying on such expedition or enterprise by all the lawful means within their power. And I require all good & faithful citizens, and others within the U.S. to be aiding & assisting herein & especially in the discovery, apprehension, & bringing to justice, of all such offenders, and in the giving information against them to the proper authorities.

"In testimony whereof I have caused the seal of the U.S. to be affixed to these presents & have signed the same with my hand. Given at the city of Washington on the 27th day of November 1806 and of the sovereignty & independence of the U.S. the 31st."

BIBLIOGRAPHY

ABERNETHY, THOMAS PERKINS. *The Burr Conspiracy*. New York: Oxford University Press, 1954.

ADAMS, CHARLES FRANCIS, see ADAMS, JOHN.

ADAMS, HENRY. *History of the United States during the Administration of Thomas Jefferson.* 2 vols. New York: Albert and Charles Boni, 1930.

————. *John Randolph*. Boston: Houghton Mifflin Company, 1898.

ADAMS, JOHN. *Works of John Adams, Second President of the United States.* Edited by Charles Francis Adams. 10 vols. Boston: Little, Brown and Company, 1850–56.

ALEXANDER, DEALVA STANWOOD. *A Political History of the State of New York.* 3 vols. New York: Henry Holt, 1906.

ALEXANDER, HOLMES. *Aaron Burr, the Proud Pretender*. New York: Harper & Brothers, 1937.

ANDERSON, JOHN J. *Did the Louisiana Purchase extend to the Pacific Ocean?* New York: Clark & Maynard, 1881.

BARBÉ-MARBOIS, FRANÇOIS, MARQUIS DE. *The History of Louisiana, particularly of the cession of that Colony to the United States of America.* Translated from the French by "an American citizen." Philadelphia: Carey and Lea, 1830.

BEIRNE, FRANCIS. *Shout Treason: The Trial of Aaron Burr.* New York: Hastings House, 1959.

BEVERIDGE, ALBERT J. *The Life of John Marshall.* 3 vols. Boston: Houghton Mifflin Company, 1929.

BOWERS, CLAUDE G. *Jefferson in Power: The Death Struggle of the Federalists.* Boston: Houghton Mifflin Company, 1936.

BRADY, JOSEPH P. *The Trial of Aaron Burr.* New York: The Neale Publishing Company, 1913.

BROADHEAD, COL. JAMES O. "The Louisiana Purchase: extent of territory acquired by the said Purchase." Missouri Historical Society Collections, Vol. I, No. 13. St. Louis, 1897.

BROWN, EVERETT SOMERVILLE. *The Constitutional History of the Louisiana Purchase.* Berkeley: University of California Press, 1920.

BURR, AARON. *Correspondence of Aaron Burr and His Daughter Theodosia.* Edited by Mark Van Doren. New York: Covici, Friede, Inc., 1929.

———. *The Private Journal of Aaron Burr, during his residence of four years in Europe; with selections from his correspondence.* Edited by Matthew L. Davis. 2 vols. New York: Harper & Brothers, 1838.

CLARK, DANIEL. *Proofs of the Corruption of Gen. James Wilkinson, and of His Connexion with Aaron Burr.* Philadelphia: Wm. Hall, Jun. and Geo W. Pierie, 1809.

COOKE, JEAN G., *see* SYRETT, HAROLD C.

CORWIN, EDWARD S. *John Marshall and the Constitution.* New Haven: Yale University Press, 1921.

DAVIS, MATTHEW LIVINGSTON. *Memoirs of Aaron Burr.* 2 vols. New York: Harper & Brothers, 1836–37.

DAVIS, MATTHEW L., *see* BURR, AARON.

DUNCAN, WILLIAM CARY. *The Amazing Madame Jumel.* New York: Frederick A. Stokes Co., 1935.

FORD, PAUL LEICESTER, see JEFFERSON, THOMAS.

GAYARRÉ, CHARLES. *History of Louisiana: The American Domination.* 4 vols. New York: William J. Widdleton, 1866.

GEER, CURTIS MANNING. *The Louisiana Purchase and the Westward Movement.* Philadelphia: G. Barrie & Sons, 1904.

HAGGARD, JUAN VILLASANA. *The Neutral Ground between Louisiana and Texas.* Austin: University of Texas Press, 1942.

HAY, THOMAS ROBSON, and WERNER, M. R. *The Admirable Trumpeter: A Biography of General James Wilkinson.* Garden City: Doubleday, Doran & Company, 1941.

HONE, PHILIP. *The Diary of Philip Hone, 1828–1851.* 2 vols. Edited by Bayard Tuckerman. New York: Dodd, Mead and Company, 1889.

HOUCH, LOUIS. *The Boundaries of the Louisiana Purchase.* St. Louis: P. Roeder, 1901.

IRVING, PIERRE M. *The Life and Letters of Washington Irving.* 3 vols. New York: G. P. Putnam's Sons, 1869.

JACOBS, JAMES RIPLEY. *Tarnished Warrior: Major-General James Wilkinson.* New York: The Macmillan Company, 1938.

JEFFERSON, THOMAS. *The Writings of Thomas Jefferson,* collected and edited by Paul Leicester Ford. New York: G. P. Putnam's Sons, 1897. (Vols. VIII and IX)

JENKINSON, ISAAC. *Aaron Burr, his personal and political relations with Thomas Jefferson and Alexander Hamilton.* Richmond, Ind.: M. Cullaton & Co., 1902.

JOHNSON, CHARLES BURR. *The True Aaron Burr: A Biographical Sketch.* New York: A. S. Barnes & Company, 1902.

JONES, W. MELVILLE, ed. *Chief Justice John Marshall, a Reappraisal.* Ithaca, N.Y.: Cornell University Press, 1956.

KNAPP, SAMUEL L. *The Life of Aaron Burr.* New York: Wiley & Long, 1835.

LANGFORD, NATHANIEL PITT. "The Louisiana Purchase and Preceding Spanish Intrigues for Dismemberment of the Union." Minnesota Historical Society Collections, Vol. 9, St. Paul, 1901.

LYON, E. WILSON. *The Man who Sold Louisiana: The Career of François Barbé-Marbois.* Norman: University of Oklahoma Press, 1942.

McCALEB, WALTER FLAVIUS. *The Aaron Burr Conspiracy* and *A New Light on Aaron Burr.* New York: Argosy-Antiquarian, Ltd., 1966.

MINNIGERODE, MEADE. *Lives and Times: Four Informal Biographies.* New York: G. P. Putnam's Sons, 1925.

MINNIGERODE, MEADE, see WANDELL, SAMUEL H.

MORISON, SAMUEL ELIOT. *Life and Letters of Harrison Gray Otis.* 2 vols. Boston: Houghton Mifflin Company, 1913.

NEVINS, ALLAN, see STRONG, GEORGE TEMPLETON.

OLIVER, FREDERICK SCOTT. *Alexander Hamilton.* New York: G. P. Putnam's Sons, 1907.

PARTON, JAMES. *The Life and Times of Aaron Burr.* New York: Mason Brothers, 1858. (5th edition)

ROBERTSON, REV. CHARLES FRANKLIN. 'The Attempts to Separate the West from the American Union." Missouri Historical Society Collections, Vol. 1, No. 10. St. Louis, 1885.

ROBERTSON, DAVID. *The Trial of Aaron Burr for Treason.* 2 vols. Jersey City: Frederick D. Linn & Co., 1878.

SCHACHNER, NATHAN. *Aaron Burr, a Biography.* New York: Frederick A. Stokes Co., 1937.

————. *Alexander Hamilton.* New York: D Appleton-Century Company, 1946.

————. *Thomas Jefferson, a Biography.* New York: Thomas Yoseloff, 1951.

SCHURZ, CARL. *Henry Clay.* 2 vols. Boston: Houghton Mifflin Company, 1887.

SHEPARD, W. R. "Wilkinson and the Beginnings of the Spanish Conspiracy." *American Historical Review,* Vol. IX.

SHREVE, ROYAL ORNAN. *The Finished Scoundrel: General James Wilkinson.* Indianapolis: The Bobbs-Merrill Company, 1933.

STEVENS, WILLIAM OLIVER. *Pistols at Ten Paces: The Code of Honor in America.* Boston: Houghton Mifflin Company, 1940.

STRONG, GEORGE TEMPLETON. *Diary.* 4 vols. Edited by Allan Nevins and Milton Halsey Thomas. New York: The Macmillan Company, 1952.

SYRETT, HAROLD C. and COOKE, JEAN G., editors. *Interview in Weehawken: The Burr-Hamilton Duel, as told in the Original Documents.* With an introduction and conclusion by Willard M. Wallace. Middletown, Conn.: Wesleyan University Press, 1960.

THOMAS, MILTON HALSEY, see STRONG, GEORGE TEMPLETON.

TODD, CHARLES BURR. *The True Aaron Burr: A Biographical Sketch.* New York: A. S. Barnes & Company, 1902.

TUCKERMAN, BAYARD, see HONE, PHILIP.

VAN DOREN, MARK, see BURR, AARON.

WALLACE, WILLARD M., see SYRETT, HAROLD C.

WANDELL, SAMUEL H. and MINNIGERODE, MEADE. *Aaron Burr.* 2 vols. New York: G. P. Putnam's Sons, 1927. (4th edition)

WERNER, M. R., see HAY, THOMAS ROBSON.

WILKINSON, JAMES. *Memoirs of My Own Times.* 3 vols. Philadelphia: Abraham Small, 1816.

INDEX